Saltwater Foodways
Companion Cookbook

by Sandra L. Oliver

Mystic Seaport
75 Greenmanville Ave., P.O. Box 6000
Mystic, CT 06355-0990
www.mysticseaport.org

Designed by Trish Sinsigalli LaPointe, LaPointe Design
Printed through Colorcraft Limited, Hong Kong

ISBN (cloth) 978-0-939511-24-2

Oliver, Sandra L. (Sandra Louise), 1947-
    Saltwater foodways companion cookbook / by Sandra L. Oliver—1st ed.—Mystic, CT :
Mystic Seaport, ©2008.
    p. : ill. ; cm.
    Includes index.

1. Cookery, American—New England style. 2. Fireplace cookery. I. Mystic Seaport. II. Title.

    TX715.2.N48 O4 2008

Contents

Introduction

THE PAST IS A TERRIFIC SOURCE OF GOOD IDEAS FOR DINNER and great tasting recipes. When *Saltwater Foodways: New Englanders and their Food at Sea and Ashore in the Nineteenth Century* first appeared over ten years ago, so many people commented on how good some of the old recipes tasted. With the great influx of interesting ethnic dishes and ingredients, we have become accustomed to eating Mexican on Monday, Thai on Tuesday, and anything you can imagine on Wednesday. Now we can put good old-fashioned New England coastal cooking back on the schedule with this collection of primarily nineteenth-century recipes.

Most people will describe these dishes as classic comfort food. A few have been inserted because they are interesting to read, and only the most courageous cooks may wish to give them a try. They were originally incorporated in *Saltwater Foodways* to illustrate life in the 1800s at sea and ashore. When a historic story mentioned a particular dish, I found a recipe to match and wrote them in such a way that the reader could prepare the dish as closely as possible to the original so that a taste of the past would clearly come through. In this book, less emphasis is on strict historic authenticity and more on pleasing the modern palate. Many recipes are hardly altered, but a few contain ideas for enlivening the dish, or modifying it to please anyone in the family.

Because so many people cook recreationally in their fireplaces, certain recipes particularly suited for fireplace preparation have specific instructions for hearthside cookery and a chapter with fireplace cookery basics are also included. Bear in mind that you can fix almost anything in a fireplace, from canned soup to grilled pizza, and historic recipes are not required to do it.

1 Cooking in a Fireplace

THE FIREPLACE

Your old house may very well have a kitchen fireplace, usually wider than a heating fireplace, with a generous hearth and often equipped with a crane. You may find a bake oven at the back of the fireplace, especially if the house was built before the 1780s. Home builders later put a more convenient oven to the side of the fireplace with its own flue leading into the chimney. Before using your old fireplace for cooking, ask a mason to check the chimney, oven, and flues to make sure the mortar is in good condition and that there are no obstructions or breaks. All chimneys and flues should be clean, and if you use your fireplace frequently, make chimney cleaning an annual custom.

You do not, however, have to have an old fireplace in order to cook in one. Modern fireplaces may be smaller and less convenient, but are suitable for many culinary operations. Fireplaces with glass doors or gas jets will be very hard to work in, so select a fireplace in your home without these features. I recommend you remove fenders, and open or remove sliding screens.

It is very likely that your fireplace will be in a living room. Cooking operations can be hard on upholstery and carpeting, so plan to clear a space around the fireplace and for your own convenience put a table nearby as a work surface.

Maintain a deep bed of ashes in the fireplace. Resist the urge to clean the fireplace frequently. The ashes form an insulating bed essential for keeping coals alive; coals will be the life of your fire and are necessary for many down-hearth operations. They are even useful for burying everything from potatoes, to eggs for baking.

THE FIREWOOD

You will need tinder, kindling, and firewood in varying sizes.

Tinder is small dry material, such as paper, bark, twigs, or pinecones which you ignite in order to set fire to larger kindling. Two or three sheets of newspaper rolled up and tied into a knot make an effective firestarter. Small sticks, twigs, and pinecones burn a little longer than paper will, and so are very good for starting fires.

Kindling varies in size from one to two inches in diameter and is ignited by the tinder. A lively blaze of kindling will set fire to larger split logs. Soft woods like pine, spruce, hemlocks, firs, and cedars, are generally unsuitable for firewood, but work well for kindling, but if you have sufficient hardwood use it instead.

Firewood for cookery needs to be hardwood—oak, maple, ash, and similar long burning woods which form long-lasting coals. Softwood can be used for certain kinds of operations such as heating ovens or quick boiling, but are not good for broiling and grilling. Creosote in the smoke from burning softwoods gives a bad flavor to food near it, as well as coating the chimney with soot. Hardwood burns more cleanly.

FIREPLACE TOOLS

Acquire a shovel, tongs, and pokers, preferably longer handled ones, and if you are going to use your oven, a long-handled shovel or peel is required for cleaning out the oven and putting food in it. Avoid grates, and consider working without andirons. Andirons take up space in the fireplace you may need for down-hearth cooking. Camping supply companies often have very useful items for open fire and fireplace cookery, and a blacksmith is easier to find than you might think. Craft shows often include blacksmiths among their artisans, and many have a line of fireplace tools and welcome special orders.

If your fireplace does not have a crane, know that you can still do boiling but a crane will make it much easier. If you have a crane, acquire a few s-shaped pot hooks in various lengths so you can adjust the distance of your pots and kettles between crane and fire.

FIREPLACE COOKING EQUIPMENT

You can consider adapting some of your regular pots and pans from the kitchen for use in the fireplace by putting them on a trivet with coals beneath them. If you plan to do a great deal of fireplace cookery invest in cast iron pots and kettles in sizes similar to the ones you use regularly in your modern kitchen. A bake kettle, or Dutch oven, is handy—a footed, straight-sided kettle with a flat, lipped lid onto which you shovel coals. A bean pot or terra cotta cook-pot will be useful. A footed frying pan is nice to have, but a regular, flat-bottomed cast iron fry pan can be set on a trivet for the same effect. Hanging griddles are also available. A gridiron or grill is good for broiling. You can use a simple grilling rack resting on a pair of bricks or acquire a more sophisticated one which clips to andirons. Similarly, you can adapt barbecue spits or acquire an antique or reproduction. Andirons with hooks on the vertical shanks will support spits. Reflective roasters and ovens are very nice, sometimes costly, and are tremendously useful for the dedicated hearth cook. Pot lifters, potholders, and long-handled utensils like forks, ladles, spoons and spatulas, like those devised for barbecues, are useful.

BUILDING A FIRE IN FIREPLACE AND OVEN

Cooking on an open fire takes a bit of practice, but is not difficult. Modern cooks mainly have to become more aware of how heat changes as the fire burns. Learning to pay attention may be the hardest part. If you are not a practiced fire builder, plan to build a couple of fires and maintain them for a while before you attempt to cook on one.

Place tinder on the ashes and lay a little kindling around it. Light the fire and let it burn briskly, adding more kindling gradually. Then add firewood, smaller pieces at first, then larger ones. While it will take about an hour before you have coals for down-hearth cooking, or a mature enough blaze for roasting, there is plenty of over-fire cooking you can do, like boiling soup, vegetables, and puddings, or frying. Plan on keeping a blaze going at the back or at the side of the fireplace with plenty of fresh wood to make a continuous supply of coals.

If your fire seems smoky, it is probably because it is not getting enough air. Adjust the fuel to open up the fire a little and when adding fresh wood, make sure you do not smother the fire with it.

Fireplace ovens need an hour to two to heat sufficiently for baking. Build your fire directly on the oven floor and underneath the curved dome of the oven ceiling. Much lively flame filling the entire oven is better than a steady burning moderate fire in the center. You can use pieces of small, lighter wood, and just keep adding fuel. When the fire has been burning for at least an hour and a half to two hours and the oven ceiling is covered with white ash, it is hot enough for baking. Spread the coals out over the oven floor and close the oven up for about ten minutes. Then, working quickly, shovel out the coals and put them into the fireplace. Swish a damp broom over the oven ceiling and place an oven thermometer inside to monitor the heat. The oven will start out at a high temperature and drop gradually giving you a wide range of baking temperatures for various baked goods, starting with breads and ending with baked beans or at its lowest warmth, drying herbs.

Bear in mind that if you are cooking in your fireplace, you should be nearby and can step on any sparks that fly out. You can put the fire screen away for the duration. Don't forget you will need to use a potholder to lift or move pots. In past times, the most common fireplace accident was a pot of hot water tipping over and scalding the cook's feet or shins. Learn how to move around the hearth without stepping on your cookware or accidentally kicking a pot or kettle.

A FEW BASIC TECHNIQUES

Roasting

You can go the high-tech or low-tech route with roasting. Historically, many devices were created for holding a roast of meat in front of a fire. Spits were hand-turned or driven by clock works. One device had vanes inside the chimney turned by rising hot air. Some reflective devices had winding mechanisms.

Antique collectors may find old roasting devices to use. If they are rusty, line them with aluminum foil, shiny side out. Modern hearth cooks can acquire reproduction tin kitchens, half-round reflective devices fitted with a spit that goes through the center. Some andirons have hooks on the inside or outside of the vertical shaft, and a spitted roast can rest on the hooks.

Make sure you start a fire at least an hour before you intend to begin roasting. You will need a good bed of coals and a steady moderate blaze. Old cookbook instructions suggest making the fire up as wide as the article to be roasted, which is still a good idea. If the roasting is going too quickly or you notice scorching, move the roasting device further from the fire until the fire dies down a little. Conversely, if the fire is not hot enough, move the item closer.

The simplest way to roast before a fire is to set up for string roasting. Put a hook or nail into the fireplace surround or in the ceiling and make a loop of twine long enough to reach from the hook or nail to a spot in front of the fire. Hook one end of it to the nail or hook.

If you wish to roast poultry, truss it well so legs are tied together and wings are tied flat against the body. Put a pair of eight to ten inch skewers through the bird at both ends of it, and rig a loop of kitchen twine around each end of the skewer long enough to create a handle. Run the handle through the bottom of the long loop. If you are roasting some other cut of meat, you can tie it up like a package so that it hangs vertically.

Twist the long loop to set the meat turning. It will continue to wind up and unwind largely unaided. If it should stop, wind it up again. It is a good idea to flip any roast end for end to prevent one end from drying out.

Place a pan beneath the roast to catch the drippings for gravy. Make sure you keep a cup of water in the pan so that the drips will not burn onto the pan. If you use a tin kitchen for roasting, you will want to put a cup of water in that, too, for the same reason. If you wish to roast potatoes or other vegetables under the meat, toss them in a little melted fat or oil before putting them in the bottom of the roaster or in the dripping pan, and omit the water. Remember that doing this may preclude having gravy.

Broiling or grilling

Broiling or grilling usually implies using a gridiron. With the recent interest in grilling, there are a number of devices on the market for suspending a gridiron over a fire. Otherwise you will want to acquire a gridiron or a pair of bricks and a rack to set on them. For grilling, have a mature fire, with a good amount of coals or do your grilling after you have heated an oven and have a pile of coals.

To determine how large a bed of coals you need, place the fish or meat on the gridiron and eye-ball it for size. Establish a bed of ashes larger than the arrangement of food, and on that lay coals spread widely enough that the heat exceeds the edges of the food stuff. In all likelihood you will turn the food at least once during cooking, and you can freshen the coals at that time. If dripping fat sets a little fire, merely ladle a bit of water on it to extinguish the flame.

Boiling, simmering, and frying

Simple boiling is the easiest cooking operation to perform, but it requires appropriate equipment, namely a pot or kettle with a bail handle, a crane over the fire, and hooks to hang the kettle. Pot lids are very useful and will hasten heating. Potholders are as important to have on hand as at your conventional stove. The principle at work is simply the closer to the fire, the higher the temperature. Raising the pot lowers the temperature and lowering it raises the temperature. Your fire changes, too, and so you need to be aware whether the fire has blazed up a bit or died down, and adjust your pot or the fire to maintain the temperature you want.

Simmering can be accomplished down-hearth. For sauce or gravy making, or cooking slowly, placing a footed pan over a bed of coals is the best bet. You may have to refresh the coals. Using earthen or redware pots surrounded by ashes and coals is another way to accomplish a simmering slow cookery.

Deep fat frying

Deep fat frying over fire is done just as other boiling is. A deep, iron pot hung from the crane and a slotted spoon or skimmer for removing the fried items are useful. A good light is very handy so that you can see the color of the food you are frying. Because maintaining temperature is more critical when you are making doughnuts or fritters, keep a thermometer handy and be prepared to move the pot closer to or further from the fire to maintain your desired temperature.

Pan frying is best accomplished on a hanging griddle, or by putting a frying pan on coals down-hearth.

Boiling puddings

A good pudding cloth made of a closely woven material such as muslin or linen dish toweling plus stout string to tie it up will be among the cookery accessories you will want to acquire if you plan to boil puddings. Puddings are always best put immediately into boiling water, so before beginning to mix a pudding, put a kettle-full of water over the fire to heat up.

When your pudding is mixed, take the cloth and dip it into the hot water, squeeze it out lightly, and spread it on a table or cutting board. Flour it generously and shake off the excess flour just as you would flour a baking pan. If the pudding is a loose one, drape the cloth into a bowl and pour the pudding into it, gather up the edges and leave a bit of room for the pudding to swell, tie it shut with a firm knot, leaving a bit of length to tie the bag to a spoon in case the pudding tends to sink. Put the pudding into boiling water, and make sure it is submerged but not touching the bottom of the kettle. If the pudding tends to sink, lay a wooden spoon or stick across the top of the kettle and tie the pudding to it with the extra length of string.

Baking

Be sure to read the instructions above for building a fire in the oven. Baking successfully will take practice, mainly to learn how to time the preparations to match the heating of the oven. For the first few times, try not to cook too great a variety of items.

If you are a novice, begin perhaps with a couple of pies, a pot of beans, and a pan of biscuits. Assemble the pies and beans ahead of time, and prepare the biscuits up to the point where all they need is the milk. When you have shoveled out the coals from the oven, close it up, and finish mixing and cutting out the biscuits. When you have finished that task, check the oven temperature and if it has dropped to the low 400s, you can begin loading the oven, putting the pies in first and then the biscuits. Put the beans in after you remove the pies.

If you are an experienced bread baker, you know how long it takes for your favorite breads to rise, and you can set them to rise for the last time about an hour before you expect the oven to be ready.

As you get the hang of timing, you can work toward trickier operations, such as cake baking. If you worry that your oven is losing heat, feel free to shovel some more coals into it toward the back or sides to raise the temperature, merely taking care that your baked goods do not get too close to them and scorch. You will find that cookie baking, which requires repeatedly opening the oven, will definitely need a reheated oven.

If you have no beehive oven, acquire a bake kettle, sometimes called a Dutch oven, a footed, straight-sided kettle with a flat, lipped lid. This can be pre-heated by setting it next to or hanging it over the fire. You can bake directly in it, or put a pie plate or baking dish on a low trivet inside. Set the kettle onto a bed of ashes with coals spread on it. Shovel more coals onto the lid. When the coals have died, brush the ashes off, and carefully lift the lid to check on the baked item inside, and refresh with new coals if it is necessary.

Most of the time, the varying temperature of the oven or bake kettle will not have an adverse effect on the item you are baking.

2 Soups and Stews

FROM ONE END OF THE 1800s TO THE OTHER, a handsome soup tureen graced most dinner tables even at sea, and a serving of soup was the classic way to begin a genteel meal. Here you will find soups, stews, and chowders. You can begin your meal with them, or make your meal from them, especially when you have made a sturdy chowder. The chowder recipes include early versions and later ones of both fish and clam, and a corn chowder for the vegetarians.

If you are a beginning hearth cook, a soup or chowder is a great way to get a feel for fireplace cooking. Pea and bean soups taste especially delicious when cooked over fire, and chowders do, too. To make the oyster and lobster stews, plan on using a sauté pan or heavy brass skillet set on a pile of coals down-hearth where you can conveniently control the heat and watch the progress of the dish.

TOMATO SOUP

TOMATO SOUP. Put three pints of tomatoes, stewed, strained, and sweetened, to two quarts of beef stock; add an onion, salt and pepper. Hood's Sarsaparilla vitalizes the blood.

BEEF SOUP STOCK. Take a shank of beef and cut the meat in fine pieces; take out the marrow and with a piece of butter put into a kettle; put over the fire, and when hot add the meat and cook till brown; then add the bones and sufficient hot water to cover; boil four hours; strain and set away to cool. Try Hood's Sarsaparilla this season.

From *Hood's Combined Cook Books*, by C.I. Hood & Co., 1875-1885, Hood's #1

IN THE LAST QUARTER of the nineteenth century, making soup, ketchup, or stewing tomatoes (recipe on page 119) were three common ways of preparing what is now America's favorite vegetable. Modern tomatoes have been bred to be sweeter than they were earlier so few modern tomatoes need the added sugar called for in the past.

This light, nicely flavored soup tastes better the second day. The recipe calls for stewed and strained tomatoes, but you may prefer the somewhat chunkier texture of unstrained tomatoes. Canned tomatoes are fine to use. If you decide to strain them, put the stewed tomatoes through a food mill or push them through a sieve with the back of a spoon. You may wish to use prepared beef stock, in which case add salt cautiously. While this recipe gives you the nineteenth-century flavor, add other seasonings to suit your own taste.

3 pints (48 ounces) of stewed tomatoes
2 quarts of beef stock
1 large onion chopped
Salt and pepper to taste

Put the processed tomatoes into a heavy, non-reactive soup pot, and put over medium heat. Add the beef stock and onion and mix well. Bring just to a boil and reduce heat, taste, and adjust seasonings.

Yields 10 servings.

PEA SOUP

Take one quart of split peas. Put them to soak in a large quantity of water overnight. In the morning pour off the water; put them on to boil in a gallon of water. Have a teakettle of boiling water to add, in case it becomes too thick. When the peas are very soft, pour them into a cullender, and rub them with a wooden spoon. Wash the pot that they were boiled in thoroughly, because if any of the peas adhere, they will be apt to burn. Then put them back, and let them boil slowly, over a gentle fire, till they are sufficiently thick.

Take a pound of nice salt pork; boil it in a separate kettle for an hour; then put it in with the peas, and let it boil another hour, to season them. Serve the soup in a tureen, and the pork on a dish. Have toasted bread, cut in small pieces, to eat with it.

From *Practical American Cookery and Domestic Economy*, by Miss Hall, 1855

PEA SOUP WAS A STAND-BY at sea because it combined easily stored peas and the ever present salt pork. On land, nineteenth-century New Englanders used ham bones for pea soup as well as salt pork. One cookbook suggested that the cook boil the peas with a "knuckle of boiled ham," an ideal use for that bit of leftover. But a nice piece of lean salt pork served the same purpose here as it does in baked beans, adding fat and flavor.

The "toasted bread cut in small pieces" were croutons, a common garnish for pea soup. Your family may not enjoy eating slices of boiled salt pork, even if it is lean, though the first boiling will reduce the fattiness somewhat. I have halved the amount needed; feel free to discard it. Better yet, use the bone from a ham with a bit of meat still on it.

Since this recipe yields close to a gallon of soup, you may wish to halve the recipe and start with two cups of split peas. Season to your taste.

**2 pounds of dried split peas,
   soaked overnight**
1 gallon of water
**8 ounces of lean salt pork,
   or a ham bone with meat**
1 large onion, chopped finely
1 stalk of celery, chopped finely
Salt and pepper to taste
Red pepper (optional)
**4 slices of bread, toasted and
   cut into croutons**

Soak the peas overnight covered generously with water. In the morning, drain and put them in a large soup pot with a gallon of water, the ham bone or salt pork, the onion, and celery. Simmer until the peas are very soft, about four hours, stirring occasionally to prevent sticking and adding more hot water to maintain a soupy consistency. You can break up the peas by mashing them against the side of the pot with a spoon or pushing them through a colander. You can also ladle out some of the peas, allow them to cool before pureeing them in the food processor, and then add them back to the soup. Pick the ham off the bone and return meat to the pot. Taste and adjust seasoning with salt, pepper, and red pepper, if desired. Sprinkle the croutons in the individual soup bowl and ladle the soup over them.

Yields 1 gallon soup or 16 one-cup servings.

BEAN SOUP

Soak a quart of navy beans overnight. Then put them on the fire, with three quarts of water; three onions, fried or sautéed in a little butter; one little carrot; two potatoes, partly cooked in other water; a small cut of pork; a little red pepper; and salt. Let it all boil slowly five or six hours. Pass it through a colander or sieve. Return the pulp to the fire; season properly with salt and cayenne pepper.

A very good soup can be made from the remains of baked beans; the brown baked beans giving it a good color. Merely add enough water and a bit of onion; boil it to a pulp and pass it through the colander.

If a little stock, or some bones or pieces of fresh meat are at hand, they will also add to the flavor of bean soup.

From *Practical Cooking and Dinner Giving*, by Mrs. Mary F. Henderson, 1882

THE INGREDIENTS FOR THIS SOUP were readily available on board ship and in most homes. When Mrs. Henderson calls for a "small cut of pork," we can probably assume salted meat since that was used in most pea and bean soups. You could also use fried bacon chopped up and added, or small pieces of ham. The suggestion of using leftover baked beans is a good one, and in fact, if you wanted this soup in a hurry, you could use canned baked beans with some sauce rinsed off to keep the soup from being too sweet.

Pushing the beans through a colander is one way of pureeing without a food processor. Though colanders appear in ship's outfitting lists, I doubt this procedure was frequently done at sea; instead, to thicken the soup, the cook allowed the beans to cook until they fell apart.

2 tablespoons butter
3 onions
3 quarts of water or beef stock
4 cups navy beans, soaked overnight
1 carrot, diced
2 medium potatoes, diced
2 ounces salt pork, chopped
1/2 teaspoon red pepper (or to taste)
Salt and pepper to taste

Melt the butter in a large soup kettle. Put in the onion and fry until soft. Add three quarts of water or stock and the rest of the ingredients and cook for several hours (2-3 minimum) or put in a slow cooker for the day. Mash the beans through a colander or process at a low speed in a processor or blender and reheat, stir to avoid sticking and add water as necessary to keep desired consistency.

Yields 1 gallon of soup or 16 one-cup servings.

BEEF SOUP

Beef soup should be stewed four hours over a slow fire. Just enough water to keep the meat covered. If you have any bones left of roast meat, &c. it is a good plan to boil them with the meat, and take them out half an hour before the soup is done. A pint of flour and water, with salt, pepper, twelve or sixteen onions, should be put in twenty minutes before the soup is done. Be careful and not throw in salt and pepper too plentifully; it is easy to add to it, and not easy to diminish. A lemon, cut up and put in half an hour before it is done, adds to the flavor. If you have tomato catsup in the house, a cupful will make soup rich.

From *American Frugal Housewife*, by Lydia Maria Child, 1833

THE ONLY VEGETABLES IN THIS SOUP are onions included for flavor, and the result looks more to the modern eye like stewed beef in a thick gravy. A dish like this is ideally suited to fireplace cookery. Even a novice can have stunning success, and the flavor of this dish cooked over fire is outstanding.

The catsup in Mrs. Child's time was different from modern catsup. Early catsup was dark and spicy, with salt, cloves, allspice, pepper, mace, garlic, and mustard seeds; it was definitely not sweet. If you want the flavor Mrs. Child intended for this dish, your best bet is to eschew commercial catsup and look in a specialty or health-food store for a low or no-sugar catsup; or substitute tomato paste thinned with water, to which you add some of the spices listed above.

1 pound stewing beef, cubed, soup bones roasted, or bones left over from roasts, steaks, ribs
1 quart of water
1 cup water
1/4 cup flour
1 dozen small onions, peeled
1/2 cup catsup
Juice of half a lemon
Salt and pepper

Put the meat and bones in a deep heavy pot (a cast-iron pot with a tight-fitting lid would be ideal) and just cover them with water. Put the lid on and stew gently for three and a half hours. Remove the soup bones. Add the onions, salt and pepper. Whisk the flour and water together and add gradually to the stew, stirring all the time. Add lemon and catsup at this time. Cook for 45 minutes. Taste and adjust seasonings.

SOUPA DA COUVAS PORTUGUESA

Take beef shank—1 lb. stew meat—Chourizo or linguica—med. size potato— 1 cup red beans either dry or canned in water drained and rinsed—add water to cover—salt to taste and simmer—When meat is tender—take out potato and mash then put back in—add minced onion—a good bunch of kale, washed and chopped fine—1/2 cup rice. Lastly 1 tablespoon pure olive oil.

From *Rose Camacho Hirsch*, May 1988

ROSE HIRSCH LEARNED THIS RECIPE from her mother, Maria Goulart Camacho, who was born at Fayal, the Azores, in 1901. Mrs. Camacho came to this country in 1918 and settled in Stonington, Connecticut, where she joined the Portuguese community, many of whom fished for a living. She brought with her the ways of cooking she had learned on her home island. Mrs. Hirsch pointed out to me that "every island had its own way of doing things," and that there are many "Portuguese" soups. On the island of St. Miguel, cabbage is used instead of kale. On others, split peas are used for soup. This red bean and kale soup is probably similar to the ones many Portuguese cooks in the New England fishing fleet made for the largely Yankee crews.

Mrs. Hirsch said that her mother used old-fashioned-style beef soup bones, and picked the meat off herself, but modern cooks may prefer to follow Mrs. Hirsch's advice and get stewing beef. You can use kidney beans if you do not find the smaller red beans in the ethnic food aisle. If you like "heat" in your soup, you may wish to choose chourizo which is the spicier of the two famous Portuguese sausages—linguica and chourizo. Plan on using a pound of sausage. Mrs. Hirsch routinely substitute two packages of frozen collards for the kale.

Beef shank bones and/or 1 pound stewing beef
1 pound chourizo or linguica sausage
1 medium-sized potato
1 cup cooked red or kidney beans
1 onion, minced
Bunch of kale, chopped
1/4 cup rice
Salt and pepper
1 tablespoon olive oil

Roast the beef bones at 350° until golden brown. Cut the beef into bite-size pieces and brown with the sausage (cut up) in a soup kettle with a little oil. Add the bones, potato, and beans, and cover with water, and simmer till the meat is tender. If you have used soup bones, remove the bones, pick off all the meat, and return the meat to the pot. Remove the potato, mash it, and return it to the pot.

Add the onion, chopped kale, and rice. Cook until the rice is done. Taste and add salt and pepper to taste. Add the olive oil and serve.

Yields 4 servings.

CHICKEN GOMBO WITH OYSTERS

Take a young chicken or the half of a grown one; cut it up, roll it in salt, pepper, and flour, and fry it a nice brown, use lard or drippings, as if for fricassee. Cut up a quart of fresh green okras, and take out the chicken and fry the okra in the same lard. When well browned return the chicken to the pot and boil. Add to it a large slice of ham; a quarter of a pound will be about right for this gombo. Pour on to the chicken, ham and okra, half a gallon of boiling water, and let it boil down to three pints. Ten minutes before serving pour into the boiling soup two dozen fine oysters with half a pint of their liquor. Let it come to a good boil, and serve it with well-boiled rice.

From *La Cuisine Creole*, by Lafcadio Hearne, 1885

"GOMBOS" OR GUMBOS were soups thickened with okra, like the recipe above, or with dried and powdered sassafras leaves, called filé. Gumbo also economically used up any cold roasted chicken. If you use bone-in chicken, it will give you a better flavor, but you will have to remove the bones before serving. Hearne suggested that "Oysters, crabs, and shrimp may be added when in season."

Fresh okra may not always be available, but you can substitute frozen. The ham can be either leftover smoked shoulder or ham steak. Boil the rice separately, and at serving time put the rice in the soup plates and pour the soup over.

**1-1/2 to 2 lbs. chicken pieces, salt and
  pepper mixed in 1/2 cup flour**
Cooking oil or bacon drippings
4 cups sliced okra
Quarter of a pound of ham, diced
2 quarts hot water
12 oysters in 1 cup liquor
4 to 5 cups cooked rice

Roll or shake the chicken pieces in the seasoned flour. In the bottom of a heavy soup pot, fry the chicken in the oil or bacon drippings until it is golden brown all over, but not done through. Remove from the pot and, when cool enough to handle, remove bones and cut into bite-sized pieces. If the oil has all been taken up, add more to the same pot, and fry the okra till it is browned. Then return the chicken to the pot. At the same time, add the ham and water. Simmer uncovered until the stock has been reduced by a quarter, about an hour. Ten minutes before serving add the oysters and their liquor. Let it come to a boil, then take it off the heat. Serve over boiled rice.

Yields 8-10 servings.

If you cook this on the hearth, to prepare the rice, bring water to a boil, add the rice, and bring back up to a boil. Then take the rice off the crane and set it on a pile of coals to steam till done. Freshen the coals as necessary to keep the rice hot.

FISH CHOWDER 1845

Cut some slices of pork very thin, and fry it out in the dinner-pot; then put in a layer of fish cut in slices, on the pork and fat, then a layer of onions, and then potatoes, all cut in thin slices; then fish, onions, and potatoes again, till your materials are all in, putting some salt and pepper on each layer of onions; split some crackers, and dip them in water, and put them around the sides and over the top; put in water enough to come up in sight; boil about half an hour, till the potatoes are done; add half a pint of milk, or a tea-cup of sweet cream, five minutes before you take it up."

From *New England Economical Housekeeper*, by Mrs. E.A. Howland, 1845

THIS FAIRLY STANDARD RECIPE for fish chowder will sound and taste familiar to most people despite the fact that it is nearly as old as Mystic Seaport's whale ship *Charles W. Morgan*.

2-3 slices salt pork
1 large onion, sliced
3-4 medium potatoes, sliced
2 lbs. cod or haddock, cut into
   bite-sized pieces
2 cups hot water
6 common or pilot crackers (optional)
Salt and pepper
1 cup milk or cream

Fry the salt pork in the bottom of a soup kettle. When it is tried out, layer your ingredients as the old recipe suggests, onions first, salt and pepper sprinkled in, then potatoes and fish. Repeat until all the ingredients are used up. When everything is in the kettle, add the split common crackers, soaked in a little water, layer on the top.

Pour in hot water until it shows through the top layer of ingredients. Simmer for half an hour or until the potatoes are done. Just before serving, pour in the milk or cream and mix gently.

Yields 4-6 servings.

FISH CHOWDER 1880

Take either a cod or a haddock, weighing about 4 lbs., skin it, cut in small pieces and wash in cold water; take a scant quarter of a pound of salt pork, cut into small pieces and fry brown in the kettle in which the chowder is to be made; for a fish weighing 4 lbs., pare and slice 5 medium sized potatoes and 1 small onion; place a layer of potato and onion in the kettle, then a layer of fish, then dredge in a little salt, pepper, and flour; keep putting in alternate layers of potatoes, fish, and the seasoning until all is used; add hot water enough to cover; cover tight and boil gently thirty minutes; add a pint of milk and 6 crackers split and dipped in cold water, and cook ten minutes longer. To sharpen the appetite take Hood's Sarsaparilla.

From *Hood's Combined Cook Books*, by C.I. Hood & Co., 1875-1885, *Hood's #3*

THIS STRAIGHTFORWARD RECIPE for an unpretentious fish chowder tastes very good. The recipe above together with the earlier one preceding taught me that chowder is very flexible and now when I make it, I seldom use a formulaic recipe.

You can use nearly any kind of fish you like though for chowder I tend to prefer a white fish like cod, haddock, stripper, pollock, cusk, or hake. I plan on about one-quarter to one-third of a pound of fish per person I wish to serve, and one medium potato per person. For every two people I like to use one medium onion. Because many people today prefer to avoid salt pork, though its flavor is a distinctive part of chowder, you can use a bit of olive oil in the bottom of the soup pot. Many people prefer to add crackers at the table, though you can see that cooks formerly included crackers in the chowder making.

You can make any chowder thicker by not putting in as much water or milk, or by putting in more flour or crackers to thicken it. I prefer a chowder with a milky broth, so I do not use flour, and I make sure that I can see the added water through the top layer of ingredients before I begin to cook them.

In some parts of New England, and certainly at sea in the early days of the fishing fleet, no milk was added to the chowder, though many of us today greatly prefer our chowder with milk or cream. Some of my Maine neighbors use evaporated milk. Restaurants sometimes finish chowder with cream.

CLAM CHOWDER

THE TWO FOLLOWING CLAM CHOWDERS, one from Mystic native Fred Hermes, a chowder master in the mid-twentieth century, and the other from Marjorie Maxson Vignot, a descendant in the Mystic shipbuilding Maxson family, seem similar but have different results. The Hermes recipe is thinner than the Vignot, with a very sturdy clammy flavor; the Vignot chowder is thicker and milder even without the milk.

FRED HERMES' CLAM CHOWDER

**3 quarts quahogs, ground through
    meat grinder**
5 pounds potatoes, sliced
2 pounds onion, ground
3/4 pound salt pork, ground

Put ground-up fat pork in a large frying pan, start cooking slowly. Then grind and add onions. In a large kettle (15-quart capacity) heat water, when boiling add potatoes, while boiling start salt pork and onions—then add them to water and potatoes. Then when having cooked awhile, add the ground quahogs and their juice. Don't cook the quahogs long. While potatoes are cooking, if you need to add water, add from a hot tea kettle. Enough water ultimately to make 10 or 12 quarts of chowder.

From Fred Hermes, 1987

This recipe yields what is locally known as Stonington clam chowder, although Fred pointed out to me that it is really the old-fashioned New England clam chowder recipe that survived mostly unchanged in southeastern Connecticut and adjacent Rhode Island.

Fred's recipe makes 10 or 12 quarts, but he made chowders for large gatherings and clambakes. He said that he always bought the clams already out of the shell for his chowder.

Two important things: avoid using a food processor on the ingredients (unless you are very skilled at pulsing)—especially the clams–because it will make them too fine for an authentic chowder. And be sure to slice, not cube, the potatoes. The following will yield one gallon.

1/4 pound salt pork, ground
**2/3 pound onions
    (5-6 medium onions), ground**
**1-2/3 pound potatoes
    (4-5 medium), sliced**
1 quart quahogs, ground
2 quarts water to start

Set chowder pot on the burner with water and potatoes and begin cooking. Start frying the ground-up salt pork, and when it begins to sizzle add the onions, and cook until the onions are golden whereupon they can be added to the boiling water and potatoes. Lower the heat and cook all together for a while until the potatoes are tender.

About 15 minutes before serving, add the clams and their broth and simmer the whole mixture. Serve with crackers.

Yields one gallon.

MARJORIE VIGNOT'S CLAM CHOWDER

Marjorie Vignot supplied the instructions in a phone conversation with me for the clam chowder she recalls her father making. While her father used no exact measurements for his chowder, Mrs. Vignot estimated the amounts you will find in the recipe below.

The important things to remember are: slice the potatoes just as Mr. Maxson insisted, with a thin side and a thick side; avoid using a food processor (unless you are very skilled at pulsing) to grind the onions, salt pork, and clams because it will make them too fine.

1/2 pound fat salt pork, ground
4-5 medium onions, ground
1-1/2 pound potatoes cut thick and thin
3 cups water
1 quart shucked clams
Salt and pepper to taste

In a large kettle, fry the salt pork until it is tried out. Remove the scraps or keep them in, as you wish. Add the onions to the fat and cook until soft, then add potatoes and clam juice and enough water to cover the potatoes. Cook until the thin edge of the potatoes disintegrates; grind clams and add them. Simmer for 15 minutes. Taste and add salt and pepper.

Serve very hot with crackers and a pitcher of milk on the table for each person to add to taste.

Yields one gallon.

SMOKED FISH CHOWDER
(Cullen Skink)

MUCH "FINNAN HADDIE" AVAILABLE TODAY is made from cod, but a true Scot's cullen skink was, of course, made only from smoked haddock. A very delicious smoked-fish chowder can be made from smoked cod, haddock, or bluefish.

What follows is a interpretation of an old cullen skink recipe that can be used with almost any sort of plain smoked fish. Smoked fish vary in smokiness and saltiness, and may need to be freshened, that is, soaked in cold water overnight, before use. The potatoes can be diced or sliced as in traditional chowders, or they can be cooked separately and mashed before adding them as in traditional cullen skink. Mashed potatoes make a creamy chowder.

---

2 lbs. smoked fish
2-3 slices of salt pork, chopped
2 medium onions
3-4 potatoes, sliced
1 cup water
1-1/2 cups milk
Salt and pepper

If necessary, freshen the fish. When it is ready, cut it into bite-sized pieces. Fry the salt pork in the bottom of a soup kettle until it is tried out. Add the onion and fry till golden. Add the potato (unless you plan to mash it) and fish. Add water until you can see it among the potatoes. Cook until the potatoes are done.

Just before serving, add the milk, and bring the chowder up to a simmer. If you mashed the potatoes, add them at this point, mixing them in well and adjusting the consistency with hot water, if necessary. Taste for seasoning and add salt and pepper if needed.

Yields 4 servings.

CORN CHOWDER

1 quart of grated corn
2 tablespoonsful of flour
4 good-sized potatoes
1 pint of milk
2 medium-sized onions
6 water crackers
1/2 pound of bacon or ham
Yolk of one egg
1 large tablespoonful of butter
1/2 pint boiling water

Pare and cut the potatoes and onions into dice. Cut the bacon or ham into small pieces and put it in a frying pan with the onions and fry until a nice brown. Put a layer of potatoes in the bottom of a saucepan, then a sprinkling of bacon or ham and onion, then a layer of corn, then a sprinkling of salt and pepper, then a layer of potatoes, and so on, until all is in, having the last layer corn. Now add the water and place over a moderate fire and simmer for twenty minutes. Then add the milk. Rub the butter and flour together and stir into the boiling chowder. Add the crackers broken; stir, and cook five minutes longer. Taste to see if properly seasoned, take it from the fire, add the beaten yolk of the egg and serve.

From *Mrs. Rorer's Cookbook*, by Mrs. S.T. Rorer, 1886

CORN CHOWDER RECIPES are fairly rare until the end of the nineteenth century, and appear less frequently than corn soup recipes. What makes this a real chowder is the presence of bacon, potatoes, onions, crackers, and milk, and the characteristic layering of ingredients. Corn seems to have stood in for shellfish from time to time, as in this recipe and in the one for corn oysters (see page 112).

When you try this recipe, keep in mind that you will probably need 12 ears of corn to give you a quart of grated corn.

Otherwise, the recipe above is very modern in its measurements and is clear enough to use without further explanation.

The yield is about a gallon. It is very thick chowder, even before you add the crackers, flour, butter, and egg yolk. You may wish to thin it out with additional milk or leave out some part of the thickeners.

Yields one gallon.

OYSTER SOUP

NO. 16. WHITE OYSTER SOUP

Separate the oysters from the liquor, and to each quart of liquor add one pint of rich milk; set it upon the fire, let it come to a boil; add the oysters; mix a heaping table-spoonful of flour with a table-spoonful of butter, and stir it into the liquor as soon as it boils; season with a little salt and pepper; serve on sippets of buttered toast.

From *The Practical Cookbook*, by Mrs. Bliss, 1864

THE LINE BETWEEN OYSTER SOUP and oyster stew was sometimes a fine one in the nineteenth century, with variations occurring in the amount of liquid and manner of thickening. Mrs. Henderson's 1882 *Practical Cooking and Dinner Giving* said "An oyster soup is made with thickening; an oyster stew is made without it," but not all nineteenth-century recipes bear this out.

Some oyster-soup recipes omitted milk, using the oyster liquor for a broth, resulting in a fairly homely dish. This recipe with milk is more attractive. Mrs. Henderson also suggested that oyster crackers and pickles were often served with an oyster soup, especially if it was the first course of dinner.

For "rich milk" you may wish to use whole milk or even half-and-half.

1 pint oysters
1 cup half milk and half cream
1 tablespoon butter
2 rounded teaspoons flour
Salt and pepper

Separate the oysters from their liquor and reserve the liquor, adding milk and cream to make one cup. Heat this in a heavy pan over a medium flame. Rub together the butter and flour in a small bowl, and add to it some of the heated milk and liquor mixture, stirring until it is blended. Return it to the pan, cooking all together for about three minutes. Add the rest of the milk and cream, and when it is hot add the oysters and cook only until their edges curl. Salt and pepper to taste. Serve with oyster crackers.

Yields two to three servings.

OYSTER STEW

Put a quart of oysters on the fire in their own liquor. The moment they begin to boil, skim them out, and add to the liquor a half pint of hot cream, salt and cayenne pepper to taste. Skim it well, take it off the fire, add to the oysters an ounce and a half of butter broken into small pieces. Serve immediately.

From *Practical Cooking and Dinner Giving*, by Mrs. Mary F. Henderson, 1882

THIS RECIPE FROM MRS. HENDERSON is fairly typical of most modern oyster stews. To understand why this stew doesn't have vegetables, think about the cooking process which cooks the oysters by stewing them. The recipe is more about the verb to stew than the noun, stew.

1 quart shucked oysters in their liquor
1 cup cream
Salt
Cayenne
3 tablespoons butter (or less to taste)

Put the oysters in their liquor into a heavy bottomed two quart pan, and heat it until you observe the edges of the oysters curl. Meanwhile warm up one cup of cream until it is hot but not boiling. Add the cream to the oysters, seasoned to taste with the salt and cayenne. Cut the butter up in small pieces and float it in the oyster stew.

Serve with crackers in the soup plate, or oyster crackers sprinkled on top if you prefer.

Yields 4 servings.

STEWED LOBSTER

Cut the lobster in pieces about an inch square. Place them in a stew pan, and over them pour a cup of water; put in butter the size of an egg; pepper and salt to the taste. Mix also with the green dressing of the lobster, and stir it about ten minutes over the fire. Just before taking off, add two wineglasses of port or sherry. Let it scald, but not boil. Hood's Sarsaparilla cures biliousness.

From *Hood's Combined Cook Books*, by C.I. Hood & Co., 1875-1885, Hoods #1

HERE IS A DELICIOUS LUNCHEON soup or an appetizer. You can increase it to dinner portions if you allow one lobster per person. You can make this from cooked lobster meat. Court bouillon, or even vegetable bouillon, is better than mere water to warm the meat in. Many people do not regard "the green dressing" or what we call tomalley as safe to eat anymore, and you will want to consider where your lobster is from before you decide what you want to do. I have reduced the amount of butter somewhat and I recommend sherry over port.

3 cooked lobsters, meat picked out
and cut into bite-sized pieces
1 cup court or vegetable bouillon
Tomalley (optional)
4 tablespoons (or 1/2 stick) of butter
1/4 cup of dry sherry
Salt and pepper to taste

Put the lobster meat in a large sauté pan, and pour the bouillon over it, adding more if you have several lobsters. Heat it over a medium heat till it is hot but not boiling, shaking it from time to time. Add the butter and allow it to melt, then stir in the sherry, and let it get very hot again. Add salt and pepper to taste. Serve on pieces of toast.

Serves four as an appetizer or luncheon.

LOBSTER STEW

The following is a variation on the Oyster Stew recipe and is my family's favorite way to have lobster stew. We usually acquire lobster at the end of the season, and cook, pick, and freeze it in milk and use the milk for the stew. I fry pieces of bread in butter or olive oil to pour the lobster stew over in the dish.

1 tablespoon of butter per person
1 shallot, chopped finely
Meat of one lobster per person
1 cup of milk per person
1/4 cup of cream per person
Salt and pepper
Dry sherry

Melt the butter in a large heavy sauté pan, and briefly cook the shallots over medium until they are soft. Add the lobster meat to the pan and heat it until it is hot through. Warm the milk and cream in a separate pan, and add to the lobster meat. Allow to come to a simmer, then add salt and pepper, and the sherry, at least a tablespoon per person or more to taste. Taste and adjust seasoning. Serve very hot on toast, croutons, or oyster crackers. It is better the next day.

TURTLE SOUP

GREEN TURTLE SOUP (The Caterer)

> *The day before you intend to dress the turtle cut off its head; and to do this properly you should hang up the victim with its head downwards, use a very sharp knife and make the incision as close to the head as possible. You must not be surprised at seeing, many hours after the decollation, the creature exhibit extraordinary signs of muscular motion, by the flapping of his fins. Separate the upper from the lower shell, and in this operation be very careful not to touch the gall bladder, which is very large and if penetrated would destroy the flesh over which its contents ran. Cut the meat from the breast in half a dozen pieces; abstract the gall and entrails and throw them away at once. Separate the fins as near the shell as possible, abstract the green fat and put it on a separate dish from the white meat. Boil the upper and lower shells in water sufficient to enable you take away the bones. Then remove with a spoon the mucilage that you find adhering to the shells; put this also into a separate dish. Into the largest stewpan your kitchen affords put the head, fins, liver, lights, heart and all the flesh, a pound of ham, nine or ten cloves, a couple of bay leaves, a good sized bunch of sweet herbs (such as winter*

savory, marjoram, basil, thyme), a silver onion cut into slices and a bunch of pars-
ley. Cover all these with the liquor in which you have boiled the shells and let it
simmer till the meat be thoroughly done, which you can ascertain by pricking with
a fork and observing if any blood exudes; when none appears, strain the liquor
through a fine sieve and return it to the stewpan, which may remain at some dis-
tance from the fire. Cut the meat into square bits of about an inch. Put the herbs,
onion, etc., into a separate saucepan with four ounces of butter, three or four
lumps of sugar and a bottle of Madeira; let this boil slowly. Whilst this is doing,
melt in another saucepan half a pound of fresh butter and, when quite dissolved,
thicken it with flour, but do not make it too thick, and then add a pint of the liquor
from the shells; let this boil very gently, , removing the scum as it rises. When both
these saucepans are ready, strain the contents of the first through a sieve, and this
done, add both to the stewpan. Warm up the liquor from the shells, the green fat
and mucilage and put them and the meat into the stewpan with the yolks of a
dozen hard-boiled eggs, the juice of half a dozen green limes and two teaspoons
of cayenne. Gently warm up the whole together, and you may regard your cook-
ery as complete.

From *Mrs. Rorer's Philadelphia Cook Book, 1886*

NOT A MOMENT TOO SOON. I offer this astonishing recipe for your interest only because in many places, sea and green turtles are endangered and are now protected from being made into soup. And cooks are protected from having to make it. Turtle soup was for a while very fashionable, enough so that there were recipes for mock turtle soup and the record shows it was made aboard ship from time to time.

Personally, I think the cook deserved to add the bottle of Madeira to himself or herself instead of the soup. Not only does turtle soup create a scene of violence and an unsavory mess, but you use practically every pan in the kitchen. Since this soup was made on board ship, surely the cook cut some corners to produce this delicacy; but, unfortunately, I have found no record yet to tell us how.

3 Breads, Yeasted and Quick

A MEAL WITHOUT SOME KIND OF BREAD was nearly unthinkable as long as a nineteenth-century family had the resources for it. City and town dwellers could buy their bread at bakeries, but many New England women—and stewards at sea—made fresh bread a couple times a week. At the beginning of the century, cooks baked bread in fireplace ovens of brick and stone, casting their round loaves directly on the floor of the oven. For the occasional johnnycake or pan of yeasted or soda biscuits, a cook might choose the bake kettle set on the hearth next to the fire with coals heaped on top. By the end of the century nearly everyone had switched to wood or coal burning stoves and baked loaves in pans set on oven racks.

If you have a fireplace bake oven you will want to use it.

TO MAKE YEAST

Put 2 quarts of water and 2 tablespoonfuls of hops on to boil. Pare and grate 6 large potatoes. When the hops and water boil, strain the water on the grated potatoes, and stir well. Place on the stove and boil up once. Add half a cup of sugar and one fourth of a cupful of salt. Let the mixture get blood warm; then add one cupful of yeast, or one cake of compressed yeast, and let it rise in a warm place five or six hours. When well risen, turn into a stone jug. Cork this tightly and set in a cool place.

From *Miss Parloa's New Cookbook and Marketing Guide*, by Maria Parloa, 1880

USE THIS YEAST in all the period recipes in this book that call for "a cup full of yeast." It is not difficult to make. Potato-based yeast was popular in the nineteenth century; there were also recipes using bran, Indian meal, rye, and other grains, and some used molasses instead of sugar. This is not a sourdough. It does not have to be fed, and should be stored tightly covered, as recommended.

Hops are easily found wherever beer and wine making supplies are sold. Cake yeast is, unfortunately, harder to find in the stores than dry because it keeps less well and is less popular than dried yeast. You can use one package of dried yeast in this recipe even though it is a slightly different yeast. I found this yeast very active in its first rising.

This recipe produces quite a lot of yeast, about three quarts, but it keeps well (I had no trouble keeping it for more than a month) and if you bake frequently you could easily use it up. The recipe is easily halved. Be sure to keep a cupful to start the next batch.

2 quarts of water

4 tablespoons of hops

6 large potatoes, pared

1/2 cup sugar

1/4 cup of salt

1 cake compressed yeast or 1 tablespoon of dried yeast

Bring the water and hops to a boil in a pot. Grate the potatoes into a separate large kettle, and when the hops and water have boiled, strain the mixture into the potatoes and discard the hops. Stir it well, and bring it to a boil then remove from the heat and allow it to cool enough that you can tolerate a spoonful on your open hand. Then stir in the sugar, salt, and yeast and mix it thoroughly.

Let it stand in a warm room for four to six hours. You will see bubbling and the mixture will expand somewhat. When it ceases activity, stir it down, and put into a glass jar with a tight lid for storing in the fridge until needed.

HOW TO SET A SPONGE

To use your own potato yeast, you will need to set a sponge. A sponge is merely a garden for growing yeast and is incorporated into the loaf you produce. All you need to provide is a bowl, a warm spot, a cup of the liquid yeast, additional warm water, and some of the flour from the bread recipe.

Put one cup of the yeast into a bowl. Add a cup of warm, but not hot, water, and mix. Stir in two cups of flour gradually and mix well. Cover the bowl with a damp towel and set the bowl somewhere warm for an hour or two. Check it and look for a bubbly surface and evidence of expansion. If you do not see it, return the bowl to the warm spot and check again later. If you find a well-bubbled surface, add another cup or two of flour and enough warm water to keep the consistency like a cake batter.

When you have used about a third of the flour called for in the bread recipe, you can use the sponge to finish the bread.

If you never achieve bubbles in your sponge it may be because it was set in too cool a place, or it had too little liquid, or that the yeast was dead. You can boost the activity by adding a teaspoon of dry yeast.

BAKING BREAD IN A FIREPLACE OVEN

In past times, the cook set the sponge for bread to rise early in the morning of a baking day in summer, and in cold weather, the evening before. Timing is everything when using a beehive oven, and you grow accustomed to the process merely by repetition and observation.

Because the oven takes from one and half to three hours to heat, depending on the weather, wood, and oven itself, it is best to plan to have your final loaves rising when the oven is half heated. You can hasten or retard the process by moving the rising loaves closer to or farther from a source of heat. It is better to let the loaves rise slowly at first, and gradually increase the heat as the time comes for them to be baked.

Beginning fireplace cooks may prefer to bake their bread in bread pans at first, then gradually accustom themselves to making cast loaves, that is, loaves shaped by hand and allowed to rise on a floured board, slipped directly or cast on to the oven floor to bake with a peel.

Freshly heated ovens will start out at a high temperature and gradually decline, an ideal situation for bread.

THIRDED BREAD

Some people like one third Indian in their flour. Others like one third rye; and some think the nicest of all bread is one third Indian, one third rye, and one third flour, made according to the directions for flour bread. When Indian is used, it should be salted, and scalded, before the other meal is put in. A mixture of other grains is economical when flour is high.

Flour bread should have a sponge set the night before. The sponge should be soft enough to pour; mixed with water, warm or cold, according to the temperature of the weather. One gill of lively yeast is enough to put into sponge for two loaves....About an hour before your oven is ready, stir in flour into your sponge till it is stiff enough to lay on a well floured board or table. Knead it up pretty stiff, and put it into well greased pans...Common sized loaves will bake in three quarters of an hour. If they slip easily in the pans it is a sign they are done.

From American Frugal Housewife, by Lydia Maria Child, 1833

LYDIA MARIA CHILD wrote, "It is more difficult to give rules for making bread than anything else; it depends so much on judgment and experience." As the directions above demonstrate, an early recipe often consists of little more than guidelines and advice.

Thirded bread is heavy, crusty, and flavorful, best eaten as an accompaniment to soups, stews, chowders, and baked beans. The following is my attempt to provide rules for what I agree is the "nicest of all bread." Bear in mind that this bread is sticky when you knead it and will be hard to handle.

To set the sponge:

3 cups lukewarm water
1/2 cup molasses
1 tablespoon or 1 package dry yeast
3 cups whole wheat flour

Mix the water, molasses, and yeast in a warm bowl and let stand until the yeast begins to foam. Stir in the flour, and beat until the batter is smooth, about 100 strokes. Cover with a damp towel and set in a warm place; allow to rise till the batter is doubled, about an hour.

To scald the Indian meal:

3 cups stone-ground white cornmeal (Indian)
2-3 cups boiling water
1 tablespoon salt

Mix the cornmeal and salt together in a large bowl. Add the boiling water and stir to prevent lumps, until you have a fairly loose mixture. Let stand until mixture cools, about 20 minutes, or until the sponge has developed.

To make the bread:
3-4 cups rye flour
1-2 cups whole wheat flour

When the sponge is ready, fold the rye flour in one cup at a time, using the back of a spoon. Spoon the scalded meal onto the rye and sponge mixture, using the back of a spoon to work the Indian meal into the dough, until the Indian is mixed evenly throughout. The dough will be very sticky, moist, and grainy in texture.

Dust a board with wheat flour, turn dough out onto it, and sprinkle more flour on the top. Knead, adding more flour as needed (it may take up to 2-1/2 cups of flour) until the dough is semi-elastic. It will still be sticky and grainy:

expect the dough to cling to your hands. Set to rise, covered, in a warm place.

When doubled in bulk, after about an hour, punch it down. Divide dough into two portions, knead, and shape into loaves. Put into greased loaf pans (or on a baking sheet or baking stone sprinkled with cornmeal). Set to rise. Preheat oven to 375°.

When doubled, bake at 375° for ten minutes, reduce oven to 325° and bake for another 40 to 50 minutes, or until the loaves come out of the pans easily.

Yields two loaves.

WHITE BREAD

To make the bread:

Ingredients:

Flour, one and a half cupfuls of yeast, lukewarm water, a table-spoonful of lard, a little salt.

Put two quarts of flour into the bread-bowl; sprinkle a little salt over it; add one and a half cupfuls of yeast, and enough lukewarm water to make it a rather soft dough. Set it one side [sic] to rise. In winter, it will take overnight; in summer, about three hours. After it has risen, mix well into it one table-spoonful of lard; then add flour (not too much), and knead it half an hour. The more it is kneaded, the whiter and finer it becomes. Leave this in the bread-bowl for a short time to rise; then make it into loaves. Let it rise again for the third time. Bake.

From Practical Cooking and Dinner Giving, by Mrs. Mary F. Henderson, 1882

THIS BREAD IS MADE by setting a sponge (like thirded bread above) using liquid yeast (see recipe page 33) which is slower-acting than modern dried or cake yeast—as you will see when you try the recipe. Mrs. Henderson said to "knead it for half an hour," which I do not think is literally necessary, though sometimes it seems like a half hour when you are doing it. Knead it until the dough is smooth and elastic and springs back when you poke it with your finger. The length of time spent will depend more on the flour and your kneading technique than anything else.

The bread is worth the wait during the risings. It has a smooth texture and chewy crust. Here is an interpretation.

10-11 cups of flour
1 tablespoon salt
1-1/2 cups yeast
2-1/4 cups warm water
1 tablespoon lard or vegetable
shortening

Set the sponge: mix the yeast and the water, then add salt and 4 cups of flour to make a soft dough or a very thick batter. Set in a warm place. When it has doubled in bulk and has a light appearance, about 4 to 5 hours (if in a warm place), melt the lard, cool it slightly and mix it into the dough; mix in an additional 3-4 cups of flour until the dough is stiff enough to handle.

Turn out onto a floured surface and knead, using up to one more cup of flour, until the dough is smooth and elastic. Let rise till doubled (about 2 hours). When doubled, punch it down, knead a bit more, and shape into loaves. Put the loaves into greased bread pans and set to rise again until doubled (about 2 hours).

When the loaves have doubled, bake in a 375° oven for 1 hour, until the loaves are golden and sound hollow when tapped.

Yields 3 loaves.

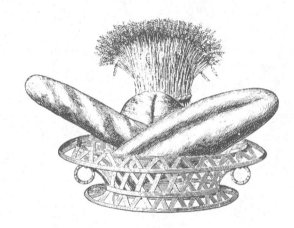

GRAHAM BREAD

Two cups Graham flour, two tablespoons molasses, one teaspoon salt, one coffee cup of scalded milk, one coffee cup of water, one-half yeast cake, enough entire wheat to thicken. Mix over night, knead in the morning, then put into pans and raise an hour. This makes two loaves.

From Rhode Island WCTU Recipe Book, recipe by Mrs. Henry Bates, 1905

THIS MAKES VERY FLAVORFUL, substantial bread. "Entire wheat" is what we call whole wheat. In the nineteenth century, following the encouragement of diet reformer and Temperance advocate Sylvester Graham, many people returned to using whole wheat, naming it after Graham.

This bread is slow-rising, so mixing it and allowing it to rise overnight is not a bad idea. You could also mix it in the morning to bake later in the afternoon to serve with supper.

2 cups Graham or whole wheat flour
2 tablespoons molasses
1 teaspoon salt
1 cup scalded milk
1 cup water
1/2 yeast cake or 1 cup of liquid yeast,
  or 1 tablespoon of dried yeast
1-1/2 - 2 cups whole wheat flour

Scald milk and add the cold water. When just warm to the touch, dissolve yeast cake in the mixture, or stir in another of the yeasts. Add molasses. Wait briefly to see if bubbling occurs.

Mix Graham flour and salt in a large

bowl, add milk mixture, and beat for several strokes. Add whole wheat flour, about half a cup at a time, and continue to mix, using the back of the spoon, until the flour is all mixed in and dough is stiff. Don't knead.

Let rise overnight or several hours if in a cool place, less time if in a warm place. When risen, punch down, and knead, adding as little flour as you can, until the dough is smooth and elastic. Put into one large or two small greased loaf pans. Let rise one to two hours. Preheat oven to 425°.

Bake for ten minutes at 425° then reduce oven to 350° for 45 minutes, or until the bread is golden and sounds hollow when you tap it.

Yields one large or two small loaves.

GRAHAM GEMS

One quart composed of two-thirds graham and one-third wheat flour, half a tea-spoon of salt, a dessertspoonful of sugar, one teaspoon of soda in a pint of sour milk and beat to a foam; stir this into the meal and bake in hot gem-irons. Hood's Sarsaparilla purifies the blood.

From *Hood's Combined Cook Books,* by C.I. Hood & Co., 1875-1885, High Street

---

THESE GRAHAM GEMS, a variation on muffins, come out of the oven with crisp exteriors. They are not too sweet so can be served with jam or jelly and, of course, butter. Like most muffins, they are best eaten hot. Gem pans are basically muffin pans, but in the late nineteenth century some had rectangular shapes instead of the more familiar round shapes and were most often made of cast iron. If you have an iron gem or muffin pan, by all means use it for this recipe. If you do not have sour milk, you can add a tablespoon of vinegar to the two cups of milk, stir and let stand for ten minutes.

1-1/3 cups unbleached flour
2-2/3 cups Graham flour
1 scant tablespoon salt
2 cup sour milk
1 teaspoon baking soda

Preheat the oven to 400°. If you are using an iron pan, put the pan in the oven to preheat; when it is hot, remove and grease it.

Meanwhile, mix together flours, sugar, and salt in a mixing bowl. Add soda to sour milk and stir quickly to mix. Add milk to flour mixture immediately and mix. Avoid over-mixing. Pour batter into hot, greased pan, and bake for 20 minutes.

Yields a dozen and a half gems (will vary depending on your gem pans).

FRENCH ROLLS

Take two quarts of flour before it is sifted, two tablespoonsful of lard, not quite 1/2 cup sugar, little salt, mix this together. Then take 1 cup of yeast & a pint of milk, and make a sponge—let this stand until morning—then mix in a stiff dough. Let this rise until about 1/2 past three—then knead and cut into cakes about 1/2 inch thick. Spread a thin coating of butter on 1/2 the circle & fold it over—let them rise until tea time, then bake in a quick oven 1/2 hour.

From the manuscript recipe notebook of Julia Gates, 1857-1930

FRENCH ROLLS OR BUNS are a pleasant light roll suitable for breakfast, dinner, or tea. If made overnight with a sponge, and finished up the next morning, these rolls, as Mrs. Gates noted, would be ready freshly baked at teatime, which would have been late in the afternoon or early evening. That timing depended on the ambient temperature and the use of the slower-working liquid yeast. They would, of course, rise more quickly in summer than winter.

Some of the other French roll or bun recipes of the period called for spice to be added, which makes them seem more suitable as a breakfast roll to eat with jam. You could certainly add spice to this recipe if you wished. Use the liquid yeast made from the recipe on page 32, and to hurry the dough along set it to rise in a warm place like an oven with a pilot light.

Sponge
2 cups milk
2 cups flour
1 cup liquid yeast or 1 package dry yeast

Make a sponge as follows: scald the milk, cool to lukewarm, then mix together with the flour and yeast. Beat it till smooth. Set aside to work. (If overnight, let stand at room temperature. If mixing it in the morning, put in a warm place.) It is ready when it has a foamy, light appearance (about 4 hours in a warm place).

Dough
4-6 cups flour
2 tablespoons melted shortening or lard
1 teaspoon salt
Softened butter

When sponge is ready, add flour, shortening, and salt. Knead, adding flour as necessary, until the dough is smooth and elastic. Let rise again until doubled, about 2 hours if in a warm place. Punch down, knead, and shape into rolls by rolling or patting out to 1/2-inch thick; cut into 2-to 3-inch rounds. Spread softened butter on half the rounds and fold over. Place on greased sheets or bake them in cast iron French Roll pans. Let rise again till doubled, about an hour, if in a warm place.

Bake in a 400° oven for 10 minutes, reduce the heat to 375° and bake for another 15 minutes.

Yields 24 rolls.

BROWN BREAD

2 cups Indian meal, 1 1/2 cups of rye meal, 1/2 cup flour, 1 cup molasses
2 cup sweet milk, 1 cup warm water, 1 teaspoonful saleratus

From the manuscript recipe notebook of Mary Miller, ca. 1850

SOMETIME AROUND THE middle of the nineteenth century the old recipe for brown bread—"rye and indian," "brown bread," and the thirded bread became what we now know as steamed brown bread. Molasses and milk were added to the familiar combination of Indian and rye meals, and a quick-rising agent replaced the yeast. When steamed, this bread was almost pudding-like and was a common accompaniment to baked beans.

Period recipes for brown bread vary in the flours and meals used. Some are made only with rye and wheat flour, or only with cornmeal and flour, reminiscent of the combinations Mrs. Child recommended for bread (see page 34). Cookbooks require steaming the bread for an average of four hours, and suggest putting it in an oven "if a crust is wanted."

You must use rye *meal*, as rye flour is much too sticky. Steam the bread in one-pound coffee cans, all-metal shortening containers, pudding molds, greased pans or even the top of a doubled boiler, greased. Aluminum foil tied over the container makes a good lid. Set the cans in a larger pot with an inch or two of hot water. The whole recipe produces a two-quart-plus-sized bread, so I have halved the recipe in the interpretation which follows.

1 cup Indian meal
3/4 cup rye meal
1/2 cup flour
1/2 teaspoon baking soda
1 teaspoon salt
1/2 cup molasses
1 cup milk

Grease the coffee cans, and get the pot of water boiling hot.

Mix together the meals, flour, and baking soda. Add the milk and molasses and blend well. Pour into the cans, filling each half full. Cover with foil, and set into the large pot. Steam 4 hours.

Yields two loaves.

SODA BISCUITS

1 pint Flour, 2 1/2 spoonsful, Cream Tartar, 1 Soda Salt, milk Peice [sic] of Butter

From an anonymous manuscript recipe fragment, ca. 1855, in the author's possession

...The success of the biscuits depends upon the even distribution of these ingredients...Pour in enough milk to make the dough consistent enough to roll out, mixing it lightly with the ends of the fingers. The quicker it is rolled out, cut, and baked the better will be the biscuits.

The biscuits are cheaper made with cream of tartar and soda than with baking powder...

From *Practical Cooking and Dinner Giving*, by Mrs. Mary F. Henderson, 1882

SODA OR SALERATUS BISCUITS were a convenience food of the mid-nineteenth century. Biscuits could be mixed and baked so much more quickly than bread—only minutes from start to finish, especially since many people were using cookstoves, the oven of which could be heated very quickly. Mrs. Beecher, among others, abhorred the rise of biscuit-eating, citing the lack of care that housewives showed by avoiding the effort to make yeasted breads for their families.

Perhaps because biscuits were so simple to make—except for very inexperienced cooks—there were few printed recipes for them, even in the later nineteenth century. The printed recipes that do exist tend to be elaborately detailed, or include other less usual ingredients such as potatoes or graham flour. The following interpretation of the anonymous recipe above produces very light biscuits.

2 cups flour
2-1/2 teaspoons cream of tartar
1 teaspoon baking soda
1/2 teaspoon salt
2 tablespoons butter
3/4 cup milk

Preheat oven to 375°

Sift together dry ingredients. Rub butter into the dry ingredients with your fingertips. Add milk about a quarter of a cup at a time, mixing with your hand or a spoon till the dough sticks together. Working quickly, roll dough out on a floured board, cut into rounds, and put on greased baking pan. Bake for about 20 to 25 minutes.

Yields twenty 2-inch biscuits.

BUCKWHEAT CAKES

One quart buckwheat flour, one handful Indian meal, four tablespoons yeast, one teaspoon salt, two tablespoons molasses—not syrup, warm water to make a thin batter. Let them rise overnight. If sour in the morning, add soda enough to sweeten the mixture.

From *Mrs. Winslow's Domestic Receipt Book,* 1876

BUCKWHEAT MAKES a heavy, even if good-tasting, pancake. Most modern recipes combine buckwheat with regular flour in order to lighten it. In the old recipe above, the added Indian meal provides a bit more crunch to the pancakes. Be forewarned: they are thin but have to be baked on a very hot griddle in order to keep them from having gummy interiors. The following recipe halves the original.

**1/2 yeast cake or 1 tablespoon
   of dry yeast
2 cups warm water
2 cups buckwheat flour
1 teaspoon salt
1/2 cup white cornmeal
2 tablespoons molasses**

Dissolve yeast in the warm water. Mix flour, cornmeal, salt together and add warm water and yeast. Stir in molasses and mix well. The batter should be thin; if you need to, add a bit more warm water. Set to rise overnight.

In the morning, heat griddle and grease it well. Pour batter and cook till pancakes are dry around edges and bubbles appear on top; turn and bake until done.

Yields four servings.

JONNYCAKES

"With jonnycakes, a lot depends on the meal. Sometimes the meal takes up a lot of water, other times not so much. We'll use two large spoonfuls of meal for each jonnycake. Salt in the meal. The water has to be hotter than anything, and put in enough to make a batter that is loose but not liquid. Some people would stop adding water now and use milk, but I know that it will be harder than a rock in a minute, so I'll dump more water in it. It's a matter of judgment. If after a couple of minutes the batter just stands right up then it is too stiff. You add the milk till you get a loose batter again.

"Some people use sugar which causes it to brown, but I don't. It browns anyway. These jonnycakes get cooked at medium but they start up at hot. You have to cook them a long time. But you can feel safe if you have company coming and they are still on the fire, because they can cook longer and it doesn't hurt them any. Use plenty of grease, bacon dripping are good and put them on by the large spoonful. Flatten them with the spatula when you turn them over. You can turn them over a couple of times. Put the done ones in the oven until they are all cooked then serve them."

Anna North Coit, interview in 1988

ANNA COIT REMEMBERS watching her Aunt Jettie Boardman make jonnycakes at the Palmer family farm in North Stonington, and still makes her jonnycakes the same way. Jettie, a nickname for Juliet, was born in 1869, and made jonnycakes in the way the Palmer family had always made them, which in southeastern Connecticut was the way Rhode Islanders made them. While not all Rhode Islanders agree on jonnycake making, it is a distinctly regional food, and in the nineteenth century accounted for the use of barrels full of meal ground from flint corn.

Earlier in the century jonnycakes were known here also (and elsewhere in New England) as bannock and were baked on a board in front of a fire.

You cannot make true jonnycakes with anything but flint corn meal, usually sold in southeastern New England as "jonnycake corn meal." And there can be no more specific a recipe than the one Anna provided above, because the meals do vary, some requiring more water, others less. About a half cup of cornmeal for two jonnycakes is a good guideline. Use boiling water. Cook them for about 15 minutes, turning them two or three times during the baking.

NEW ENGLAND CORN BREAD

3/4 cups corn meal
1 1/4 cups flour
1/4 cup sugar
4 teaspoons baking powder
1/2 teaspoon salt
1 cup milk
1 egg
1 tablespoon melted butter
Mix and sift dry ingredients; add milk, egg well·beaten, and butter; bake in
shallow buttered pan in hot oven twenty minutes.

From the *Boston Cooking-School Cook Book*, Fannie Merritt Farmer, 1896

MANY PEOPLE THINK of cornbread as a Southern dish, but a great many Yankees baked and ate cornmeal based quick breads that always tasted best fresh from the oven. This is a perfectly serviceable cornbread that you can put together quickly, and bake in a conventional stove oven, in a bake kettle, or beehive oven. Miss Farmer wrote this recipe in the late nineteenth century, in a modern style that is still in use. By using the above ingredients, you can use the slightly more specific instructions included here.

Preheat the oven to 400° and grease an eight-by-eight-inch baking pan. Sift together the dry ingredients and put into a bowl. Whisk together the egg, milk, and melted butter and add to the dry ingredients, mixing them quickly and thoroughly but not too much. Pour into the baking pan, and bake for 20 minutes until golden brown on top, and firm to the touch. Serve warm.

Serves 4-6.

4 Main Dishes

A MAIN DISH IN NINETEENTH CENTURY NEW ENGLAND, in fact, America, almost always meant meat. A formal meal called for a roasted or boiled joint or a full platter of chops or steaks as a centerpiece. By that time, too, potatoes were the usual accompaniment, and bread was served. Vegetables were a side dish and often included items like rice and macaroni that we think of today as a starch. Many families started their meal with soup, and nearly everyone who could afford it, ended with a sweet dessert. Smaller meals employed meat in pies, or in a gravy served on potatoes or toast.

Beef and pork topped the list of preferred main dish meats. Mutton, a meat that has virtually disappeared from store meat departments in this country in recent times, was reasonably common. Lamb and veal were seasonal treats, and chicken could appear on the table almost any time. Wild fowl in New England was an autumn food, and turkey was the inevitable for Thanksgiving and Christmas both.

This chapter also includes stuffing recipes and the sauces and gravies made to accompany various dishes.

Fireplace cooks can prepare almost any one of these recipes down hearth. Watch for specific advice and instructions with each recipe.

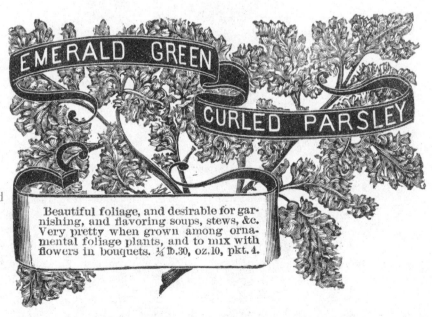

EMERALD GREEN

CURLED PARSLEY

Beautiful foliage, and desirable for garnishing, and flavoring soups, stews, &c. Very pretty when grown among ornamental foliage plants, and to mix with flowers in bouquets. ¼ ℔.30, oz.10, pkt. 4.

BEEFSTEAK

The first requirement is not so much a tender and juicy steak, though this is always desirable, but a glowing bed of coals, a wire gridiron—a stout one with good sized wires, and double so that you can turn the steak without touching it. The steak should be pounded only in extreme cases, when it is cut too thick and is "stringy." Attempt nothing else when cooking the steak; have everything else ready for the table; the potatoes and vegetables dished and in the warming-closet. From 4 minutes onward is needed to cook the steak. The time must depend on the size, and you can easily tell by the color of the gravy which runs from the steak, when gently pressed with a knife, as to its condition. If the master of the house likes "rare done," it will be safe to infer that it is done enough for him, when there is a suspicion of brown gravy with the red; if, as is generally the case, the next stage is the favorite one, remove the steak from the gridiron the instant the gravy is of a light brown. Remove it to a platter, pepper and salt to suit your taste, put on small lumps of butter, and then for two brief moments, cover it with a hot plate, the two moments being sufficient to carry it to the table. One absolutely essential factor in the preparation of good beefsteak is that it must be served at once.

From *Hood's Combined Cook Books*, by C.I. Hood & Co., 1875-1885, Hood's #2

A "GOOD MEAL" and "beefsteak" was, and is, synonymous for many Americans. The residents of most towns in coastal New England were able to buy fresh meat, certainly steak, almost anytime they wanted it. Local farmers raised cattle for market, and a steady supply came from the West to eastern cities. While a roast may have been considered the best thing for a Sunday or company dinner, beefsteaks were perfectly suitable for family weekday dinners.

The detail to which the Hood's cookbook writer, above, went to describe the proper method of grilling a steak may tell us more about how people really did cook it than how they ought to have done. Most cookbooks of the period emphasized the need for good judgment in preparing steak—from selecting the best one in the first place to the best length of time for grilling. Steak was often buttered, salted, and peppered before being served, and was not generally served with gravy. Another cookbook writer of the era said "there should be no gravy. The juice of a properly cooked steak should be in the inside of the steak, and not swimming in the dish."

You will want a gridiron or grill to cook a beef steak in the fireplace, and a mature fire with many coals. Upon a nest of ashes lay a bed of coals at least as large as your steak and place the gridiron over that. Cook the steak on one side, and turn, refreshing the coals if necessary at the time you turn it. Or use your own familiar preferred way of cooking steak.

A POT ROAST

Trim off the rough parts of a nice brisket of beef, place it in a kettle over a good fire; brown on one side, then turn and brown on the other; then add one pint of boiling water, cover and cook slowly fifteen minutes to every pound. Add salt when the meat is half done. After the water evaporates add no more....

From *Mrs. Rorer's Philadelphia Cook Book,* 1886

THE PREFERRED WAY to cook a joint of fresh meat in the hearth cooking era was to roast it before a clear bright fire, either suspended on a spit (as described on page 63) or in a tin kitchen. To put it in an oven was termed baking and was not favored. Cooking a piece of meat in a pot as described above was what we call braising but the cut of meat was called a roast, and since it was cooked in a pot, it was called a pot roast. One early way of preparing pot roast was to prepare beef a-la-mode, and required the cook to chop salt pork fat with herbs and stuff it into incisions in the beef. Cheap, tough cuts of beef became tender that way.

Modern beef is often already well streaked with fat, and hardly anyone ever adds more. The following instructions are adapted from the first American cookbook, *American Cookery,* published in 1796, and can be used either in fireplace or stove top cookery, though meat cooked long over a fire is extraordinarily good. The historic recipes recommend that the cook lay a couple of bones in the bottom of the pot on which to rest the roast to prevent it from sticking. Not a bad idea.

To prepare this in the fireplace, use an iron pot hung from a crane. Maintain a steady, mature fire without a great deal of flame, and raise and lower the pot as needed when you check the roast to turn it.

POT ROAST

**4-6 pounds of beef round, rump,
  or chuck**
A couple of slices of lean salt pork
1 large onion, quartered
2 carrots cut in three-inch lengths
2 cups of red wine
2 cups of water
Salt and pepper

Put the salt pork in the bottom of a heavy pot and try it out until it is crisp. Remove the pork if you wish. Dredge the meat with flour, and sear it on all sides in the pork fat. Lay a couple of skewers (or bones) in the bottom of the pot and set the meat on them. Put in the onion, carrots, wine, and water, and put a tight fitting lid on the pot. Put it back on the fire, and simmer for three hours, turning the meat every hour or so, and checking to see that there is still sufficient liquid.

When the meat is done, take it from the fire and put it on a platter. Pour out the gravy, straining the cooking liquid, and, if it is not as thick as you would like, add a little cornstarch or flour mixed in water, and cook it until it has thickened.

Serves six to eight.

EARLY SCARLET HORN CARROT.

This is a fine, early, short, stump root variety, large at top. Good size, fine quality, yields well, sells well.
℔. 60, ½ ℔. 35, ¼ ℔. 20, oz. 7, pkt. 3.

BOILED CORNED BEEF DINNER

Corned Beef

If dinner be at 12 or 1 o'clock, corned beef should be put on to boil as early as 7 o'clock. If boiled gently for this length of time, it will be very tender, have a fine flavor, and will cut easily and smoothly. Eat with mustard or vinegar.

From *Hood's Combined Cook Books* by C.I. Hood & Co., 1875-1885

A GOOD RULE OF THUMB for cooking corned beef is one hour of simmering for every one pound of beef. For a classic boiled dinner, follow the steps outlined below. Save the leftovers for a breakfast or supper hash. Four pounds of beef will be sufficient for eight servings.

This is the perfect dish for novice hearth cooks. All the cook has to do is pay attention to the fire and keep the pot at a gentle steady simmer, and add water as needed. The fire adds a lovely savor to the food.

BOILED CORNED BEEF DINNER

4 pounds of corned beef
1 potato per person
2 carrots per person
1 small white turnip per person
1 small onion per person
1 medium beet per person
1 wedge of cabbage per person

Put the corned beef in cold water and bring it up to a gentle simmer, and keep it at a simmer for one hour per pound of beef. Keep it covered with water by adding hot water from a tea kettle.

About an hour before serving, add turnips, and carrots, peeled and quartered, to the pot.

About three quarters of an hour before serving, add potatoes and peeled onions to the pot. If you like beets with your boiled dinner, put these on to cook whole and unpeeled, in a separate pan. Skin them just before serving.

In the last 15 minutes, add wedges of cabbage.

Remove the meat and test the vegetables with a fork to make sure they are done to your taste. Arrange all on a platter.

Serves 8.

HASH

Chop the cooked meat and twice as much potatoes, cold, in separate bowls. Put a little water, boiling, and a bit of butter into an iron saucepan, stewpan, or spider; bring to a boil. Then put in the meat and potatoes, well salted and peppered. Add other vegetables, if desired. Let it cook through well, under cover, stirring occasionally, so that the ingredients may be evenly distributed and to keep the bottom from sticking to the pan. When done, it should be not at all watery, nor yet dry, but have sufficient adhesiveness to stand on a well-trimmed and buttered toast, on which it should be served. Hash from cold poultry can be made the same way.

From *Hood's Combined Cook Books* by C.I. Hood & Co., 1875-1885

LEFTOVER MEAT was often minced or "hashed" and warmed up in gravy, a dish that was sometimes termed "minced meat" (not to be confused with mincemeat, the preserve for pie-filling) or sometimes called "hash." By the last part of the nineteenth-century it was customary to serve hash on toast—a refinement for the dining room, and not necessarily the way hash appeared for breakfast or supper at sea and ashore for ordinary folks.

Many of the early nineteenth-century cookbooks do not give hash the great detail that the recipe above does published later. The Hood cookbooks borrowed heavily from Mrs. Henderson's *Practical Cooking and Dinner Giving* for this hash recipe. In her book, Mrs. Henderson said this about hash: "Notwithstanding this distinguished dish is so much abused, I particularly like it." She went on to describe how one New York family she knew prepared it, using leftovers of large joints "purchased with special reference to this dish," and related that "Cold corned beef is generally considered best."

The amount of potatoes or vegetables in hash is, and was, up to personal taste. Chopping the meat finely could be accomplished in a wooden bowl with a chopping knife, or it could be put through a grinder. Modern people can use a food processor, but must be careful to leave recognizable pieces of meat and vegetable.

Allow about a half cup of chopped meat per serving, with as much of the cooked potatoes or vegetable as you like. If you prefer a crisp hash, then put oil on the pan and fry the hash.

This dish is easily made in a fireplace using either a griddle hanging over the fire or a fry pan on a low trivet over a bed of hot coals.

PRESSED CORNED BEEF

CORNED BEEF TO SERVE COLD (Mrs. Gratz Brown)

If it is too salt, soak it for an hour in cold water, then put it over the fire, covered with fresh cold water, four or five cloves (for about six pounds of beef), and three table-spoonfuls of molasses. Boil it slowly. In an hour change the water, adding five more cloves and three more table-spoonfuls of molasses. In two hours more, press the beef, after removing the bones, into a basin rather small for it; then, turning it over, place a flat-iron on top. When entirely cold, the beef is to be sliced for lunch or tea.

From *Practical Cooking and Dinner Giving,* by Mrs. Mary F. Henderson, 1882

TODAY CORNED BEEF is made from the rump or brisket and is boneless, but in the past other parts of the animal were also corned. And since some people were still salting their own corned beef there was variability in the product's saltiness, never an issue today. You will not need to change the cooking water. This process makes a luncheon meat suitable for picnic, lunch or tea sandwiches.

2 to 3 lb piece of corned beef
Water to cover
1 tablespoon whole cloves
1 tablespoon whole peppercorns
1/4 cup of molasses

Put the corned beef into a kettle, add water just to cover, and the cloves, pepper and molasses. Bring to a boil over a moderate heat, reduce the temperature and gently cook for one hour per pound of meat. When it is tender, remove the meat from the kettle and find a pan into which you can pack the meat. You may wish to cut it and put it into two bread pans. Set another pan on top of the meat and put a weight in the pan, using, for example, a couple large cans of vegetables or a couple of bottles of water. Allow to cool in a refrigerator. When cold, turn it out and it is ready for slicing for sandwiches.

DRIED-BEEF GRAVY

Dried Beef—Slice the beef as thin as possible; put into a saucepan, cover with cold water, and set over the fire until it slowly comes to a boil; then drain off all the water, add two gills of rich cream, if you have it, or rich milk, adding two table-spoonfuls of butter. If milk is used, wet to a smooth paste or cream a teaspoonful and a half of flour, and stir it in as it comes to a boil, and serve hot.

From *All Around the House* by Mrs. H.W. Beecher, 1878

EVEN INTO THE TWENTIETH CENTURY, as they and their neighbors had done for generations, one farm family in North Stonington, Connecticut, kept a piece of dried salted beef hung in their cellar-way from which they shaved the slices to be made into dried-beef gravy. Like salt-pork gravy, (page 59) this dish was also served on top of potatoes, toast, or jonnycakes, for breakfast or supper. In the seafood chapter, on page 85, you will find the salt fish equivalent of this and the salt pork recipe following. In some places, not usually New England, sausage is also fried and added to gravy.

Nowadays dried beef comes all rolled up in a little glass jar. Get the kind that says it is not pre-formed or chopped.

CREAMED CHIPPED BEEF

2 tablespoons of butter
4 ounces of dried beef
2 tablespoons of flour
1 cup of milk, cream,
   or half-and-half
Pepper

Melt the butter in a heavy sauté or fry pan over a low heat, and tear the dried beef into it. Stir it until the beef is warmed through. Shake the flour into the pan, and cook it briefly. Then add the milk, or cream, and stir constantly until a sauce has formed. Taste and adjust seasonings. Serve on toast or baked potatoes.

Serves two amply.

BOILED TONGUE

To dress beef tongue

To dress them, boil the tongue tender; it will take five hours; always dress them as they come out of the pickle, unless they have been very long there; then they may be soaked three or four hours in cold water; or if they have been smoked, and hung long, they should be softened by lying in water five or six hours; they should be brought to a boil gently, and then simmer until tender.

From *Practical American Cookery and Domestic Economy* by Miss Hall, 1855

COLD TONGUE was a standard offering for teas and suppers in nineteenth-century New England, served by itself or in sandwiches. It could be cooked and eaten fresh shortly after slaughtering, or it could be pickled as beef was in salt, brown sugar, and saltpetre. As the recipe above says, it was sometimes smoked as well. Today smoked tongue is the rule and if you wish to try this recipe with fresh tongue you will have to order it specially.

Beef tongue was not the only tongue eaten; veal, sheep, and lambs' tongues also appear in period recipes. Animal "spare parts" like heart, kidney, liver, tripe, lights (lungs), heads, and feet were all commonly used in the past but are hard to find on meat counters today.

VEAL PIE

Take a shoulder of veal, cut it up and boil one hour, then add a quarter of a pound of butter, pepper and salt, cover the meat with biscuit dough, cover close and stew half an hour, and it will be ready.

From *Mrs. Winslow's Domestic Receipt Book for 1871*

THIS IS MERELY A VEAL STEW with biscuit crust similar to dumplings—a pie that did not require an oven. Modern veal has less fat than other meats because of the age of the animal; in the nineteenth century veal was even leaner, which explains the quarter of a pound of butter.

Generally, stewing veal is available already boned and cut in stewing pieces.

If you cook this down-hearth, use a small bake kettle. If you prefer a crusty biscuit top, place the lid on the kettle and top with fresh coals, and bake for about 10 to 15 minutes.

VEAL PIE

1 to 1-1/2 pounds of stewing veal
Flour
2 tablespoons butter or olive oil
1 medium onion, chopped
Water
Salt and pepper
Thyme, parsley and mace

Biscuit dough (page 42)

Cube the veal, if not cut up already, dust with flour. Melt the butter or olive oil in a heavy saucepan over a medium high heat. Brown the veal, add the chopped onion, and cook till the onion is somewhat soft. Add enough water to barely cover the meat, reduce the heat to a simmer and stew for an hour. Prepare the biscuit dough. Pat it out about three-quarters of an inch thick, and cut rounds of dough. Add salt and pepper, thyme, parsley, and a shake or two of mace to the stewing veal and drop the biscuit dough on top of the stew. Close the saucepan tightly, and continue cooking covered for ten minutes, uncover for an additional ten or until the dumplings are cooked through. If you prefer, you can make a crusty biscuit top by putting the stew in a casserole, with the biscuits on top, and putting onto a hot (400°) oven for 15 minutes.

Yields 4 servings.

ROAST PORK

Shortly after pig butchering in the fall, many New Englanders had a treat of freshly roasted spare ribs, loin or rib roasts. Since pigs went to sea, and were butchered for fresh meat, roasting on shipboard was probably done in the galley stove's oven, a process, strictly speaking, called baking in the nineteenth century. Ashore some people might still have used a fireplace and tin kitchen.

For a roast, most cookbooks today recommend 25 to 30 minutes to the pound in a 325° oven. If you roast in a fireplace, your fire's heat may vary so an instant-read thermometer will give you a measure of how done your meat is. Look for an internal temperature of 165°. Spareribs will cook more quickly, especially if they have bones left in.

Applesauce is the traditional accompaniment to roast pork, and even at sea, Captain's wife Mary Lawrence commented once that a pitch of the ship dumped out some apples being stewed to accompany pork for dinner, resulting in a sauce-less roast of pork.

If you roast your pork down hearth, consider setting a small pan with peeled chopped apples in it near the fire to make an applesauce to accompany the roast.

BOILED HAM

To boil hams it should be boiled in large quantity of water-in that for a long time-one quarter of an hour for each pound: the ham is most palatable when cold-and should be sent to the table with eggs-horseradish and mustard.

From the manuscript recipe notebook of Julia Palmer, ca. 1840-60,
property of Anna North Coit, North Stonington, Connecticut

DESPITE THE FACT that Miss Palmer recorded the opinion that ham was "more palatable" when cold, a good many New Englanders ate it boiled hot for dinner. Period cookbooks give similar instructions for boiling, sometimes recommending an overnight soak to freshen it, then advising the cook to remove the skin, sprinkle the ham with cracker or bread crumbs, dot it with cloves, and put it before a fire to brown.

The directions above are for a saltier and dryer cured ham than is usually available today, unless one is buying country-cured hams, such as a Smithfield, in which case overnight soaking to reduce the saltiness is a good idea. Use your own taste and judgment after tasting a slice.

A ham can be used in a boiled dinner just as you would use corned beef (page 51). And is an easy operation in the fireplace. It is done when the meat pulls away from the bone. A garnish of eggs with cold leftover ham, and horseradish and mustard on the side, still seem like a good idea.

SALT PORK GRAVY

To Fry Pork.

If too salt, freshen by heating it in water after it is cut in slices. Then pour off the water and fry until done. Take out the pork, and stir a spoonful of flour into the lard, and turn in milk or cream enough to thicken. This makes a more delicate gravy and is very palatable.

From *The Complete Domestic Guide* by Mrs. L.G. Abell, 1853

THIS SALT PORK AND A GRAVY combination made with milk has been around for a long time, possibly before Mrs. Abell put it in her cookbook. It has endured under various names, the most common one in New England being "salt-pork-and-milk gravy." It was served over potatoes, toast, biscuits or jonnycakes as supper or breakfast. It is delicious, and, for modern sedentary people, deadly. Try it once for the experience, but be sure to use the leanest salt pork you can find.

SALT PORK GRAVY

5-6 slices lean salt pork
2 tablespoons of flour
1 cup milk or cream

Cut the salt pork in thin slices or cut up in small cubes. Fry it until it is crisp; remove the pork from the pan and drain. Pour off some of the fat, but retain two tablespoons in the pan, reduce the temperature to a medium low, and stir the flour into the fat with a whisk. Add the milk gradually, whisking to mix, and cooking until it thickens.

Serve by putting the gravy over potatoes or jonnycakes (recipe page 44) and garnishing with the pork. Or mix the pork back into the gravy and then pour over the potatoes or jonnycakes.

Serves two to three.

SALT PORK FRIED WITH APPLES OR POTATOES

Fried salt pork and apples is a favorite dish in the country; but it is seldom seen in the city. After the pork is fried, some of the fat should be taken out, lest the apples should be oily. Acid apples should be chosen, because they cook more easily; they should be cut in slices across the whole apple, about twice or three times as thick as a new dollar. Fried till tender, and brown on both sides—laid around the pork. If you have cold potatoes slice them and brown them in the same way.

From *American Frugal Housewife,* by Lydia Maria Child, 1833

A GOOD, QUICK DISH for an early-nineteenth-century breakfast or supper for hard working rural folks, this is delicious, but most modern people will shy away from the salt pork. If you decide to try it, select lean salt pork, slice it as thick as slab bacon is usually sliced, allow two slices of pork and one tart, cooking apple per person sliced a quarter of an inch or so thick.

Cold, boiled potatoes are also good fried up this way.

BOILED MUTTON AND CAPER SAUCE

Leg of Mutton—Boiled.

Do not have the mutton too fat or too large. Cut off the shank, which the butcher will have nicked for you, leaving about two inches beyond the ham. Wash and wipe carefully and boil in hot water, with a little salt, until a fork will readily pierce the thickest part. About ten or twelve minutes to the pound is a good rule in boiling fresh meat. Serve with caper sauce. Since you intend to use the liquor in which the meat is boiled for to-morrow's soup, do not over salt it. But sprinkle, instead, salt over the leg of mutton after it is dished; rub it all over with butter and set in a hot oven for a single minute.

From *The Dinner Year Book*, by Marion Harland, 1878

MUTTON, A SHEEP THAT IS over a year old, is hard to find these days by that name, unless one has sheep-raising friends. We seldom boil fresh meat or poultry these days but in the past, large joints of meat like a leg of mutton were commonly boiled. In fact, an early 1800s dinner menu might feature both a roasted piece of meat and a boiled one, each served with a gravy or sauce.

The real treat here is the caper sauce which is absolutely delicious and is wonderful for a variety of dishes including roasted chicken or turkey, and would be very good with roasted lamb which is a good deal easier to find than mutton.

CAPER SAUCE

1/2 cup butter
2 tablespoons of flour
1 pint water or chicken stock
1 tablespoon lemon juice
2 tablespoons of capers
1 teaspoon anchovy paste (optional)
Salt and pepper to taste
Cayenne (optional)

Melt the butter in a heavy saucepan, and stir in the flour and cook until it bubbles. Gradually add the water or stock, and cook it, whisking to keep it smooth, for five to eight minutes. Add lemon juice, capers, and anchovy paste. Whisk and cook a few moments longer, then taste, adjust seasonings and add cayenne if you wish.

Yields 1-3/4 cups.

MUTTON CHOPS

Mutton chops—Broiled.

Cut from the best end of the loin; trim them nicely, removing fat or skin, leaving only enough of the former to make them palatable; let the fire be very clear before placing the chops on the gridiron; turn them frequently, taking care that the fork is not put into the lean part of the chop; season them with pepper and salt; spread a little fresh butter over each chop, when nearly done, and send them to table upon very hot plates.

Mutton Chops—Fried.

The fat in which the chops are to be fried should be boiling when the chops are put into it. They should be pared of fat, and well trimmed, before cooking; they should be turned frequently, and when nicely browned, they will be done; of course, if they are very thick, judgment must be exercised respecting the length of time they will occupy in cooking.·

From *Practical American Cookery and Domestic Economy,* by Miss Hall, 1855

MUTTON OR LAMB CHOPS

Allow two small lamb chops per person, more if you have hearty eaters. You will find them already cut in the meat department of the store. If you plan to broil or grill them, remove as much of the fat as you can, and brush them on both sides with olive oil. Preheat the broiler or grill. They will cook in very little time. They may also be sautéed. Again, brush each side with oil, and have the pan hot before you put the chops on it.

To broil on the hearth, check to make sure you have a good bed of coals. Spread ashes on the side of the hearth to make a nest larger than the size of your gridiron. Trim the chops as above, and brush both sides with oil, and grease the grill. Off the fire, arrange the chops on the gridiron, and shovel some bright embers in the same diameter as the space occupied by chops on the gridiron. Set the gridiron and the chops over the coals. Watch closely, and when it is time to turn the chops, remove the gridiron, freshen the coals if they have died back, turn the chops and replace the gridiron. Remove the grilled chops to a warm platter, and serve them with caper sauce on previous page.

ROASTED CHICKEN

A smart fire is better than a slow one; but they must be tended closely.

From *American Frugal Housewife*, by L. Maria Child, 1833

DIRECTIONS FOR ROASTING CHICKENS in early cookbooks reveal that often people roasted smaller birds than we usually find sold as roasters today, and the times recommended seem short. The chickens were not always stuffed. A slice or two of buttered, salted and peppered bread may have been stuffed into the crop. The drippings were made into gravy. With the shift from fireplace roasting to stove oven roasting, cooks found that rubbing the chicken all over with butter, then dredging with flour, roasting in a very hot oven, made for moist roasted chicken. We will concentrate here on describing how to roast in your fireplace.

Prepare your chicken as you would for roasting it in a stove oven. If you do not stuff it, it will roast in a shorter time. Review the roasting-fire building instructions in chapter 1.

Whether you are using a tin kitchen or plan on putting the spit on the andirons with a dripping pan beneath, fasten your chicken to the spit with skewers. Dredge the chicken with flour and salt and place it in the tin kitchen, and set it down before the fire. Put a little water in the bottom of the tin kitchen to catch the drippings and to keep them from scorching. Until you gain some experience, and develop a knack for fire-handling,

consider using an instant-read thermometer to determine the chicken's interior temperature. Aim for 185°.

Put the giblets with water in a small pot to hang over the fire or to keep near the side of the fire. Turn the chicken about every 15 minutes, and baste it using the giblet broth. If the skin darkens too quickly, pull the tin kitchen a few more inches away from the fire, and/or let the fire die down somewhat.

If you are using the string roasting method, truss the bird, wrapping the string across and under the bird, on both sides, and hang about eight to ten inches from the fire from the crane or from a nail in the mantle or lintel. Place a dripping pan or dish beneath the chicken. Twist the string to wind it up, and watch it to make sure it continues to rewind. Baste every 15 minutes or so, as you would for a spitted bird.

It will take 20 minutes a pound on average providing you maintain a good fire. Test with the instant-read thermometer at the thigh joint, or observe that the drumstick moves freely and the juice runs clear when you poke the joint with a knife or fork.

Take the bird off the spit, or lay it on a platter and cut away the string.

GRAVY

Most people put a half pint of flour and water into their tin-kitchen, when they set meat down to roast. This does very well; but gravy is better flavored, and looks darker, to shake flour and salt upon the meat; let it brown thoroughly, put flour and salt on again, and baste the meat with about half a pint of hot water (or more according to the gravy you want). When the meat is about done, pour these drippings into a skillet and let it boil. If it is not thick enough, shake in a little flour; but be sure to let it boil, and be well stirred, after the flour is in.

From *American Frugal Housewife,* by L. Maria Child, 1833

MRS. CHILD'S METHOD described above works very well, or you can hang a small pot of water over the fire with the giblets simmering in it and use that broth to baste the bird. Add a small onion, a bay leaf, some pepper and salt, thyme, and marjoram to it, too.

As she instructs, strain the gravy from the dripping pan into a small skillet, set it on a bed of coals, add flour if needed, and cook until it is thickened, adding the giblet broth until you have enough gravy.

BROILED CHICKEN

In broiling chickens, it is difficult to do the inside of the thickest pieces without scorching the outside. It is a good plan to parboil them about ten minutes in a spider or skillet, covered close to keep the steam in; then put them upon the gridiron, broil and butter. It is a good plan to cover them with a plate, while on the gridiron. They may be basted with a very little of the water in which they were boiled.

From *American Frugal Housewife,* by L. Maria Child, 1833

BROILING, OR GRILLING as we say today, chicken is tricky. Simmering it a few minutes before grilling and covering them with a heat proof pie plate, is a good idea if you are going to broil your chicken pieces down hearth. You may baste with the cooking water, as Mrs. Child suggests, or your favorite barbecue sauce.

CHICKEN SALAD

Boil tender four good sized chickens; when cold, cut off the white meat, and chop rather coarse. Cut off the white part of celery and chop in the same manner. To two quarts and a pint of the chicken allow one quart and a pint of the celery and a spoonful of salt. Mix well together, and then stir in part of the dressing. Shape the salad in a flat dish, and pour over the remainder of the dressing. Garnish with hard boiled eggs, beets, and the tops of the celery.

From *The Appledore Cookbook,* by Maria Parloa, 1880

THIS MAKES A VERY LARGE chicken salad, and the dressing Miss Parloa mentions was a homemade mayonnaise-like dressing with whipped cream folded into it. Most people will prefer to use a commercial mayonnaise thinned to pouring consistency with cream, or you might prefer to use your favorite bottled salad dressing, like a ranch or creamy caesar.

Unlike a roast, which can come to the table in solitary splendor, a chicken salad probably seemed a little messy to the Victorian eye. Most cookbooks of the era advise garnishing with rows of capers, slices or "little cut diamonds" of hard-boiled egg, celery tufts and parsley.

CHICKEN SALAD

Meat of one cooked chicken, diced
Half as much celery as chicken, diced
Salad dressing
Hard boiled eggs
Leafy celery tops
Curly parsley

Mix the chicken, and celery all together coating the meat and celery well with the dressing. Taste and adjust for salt and pepper. Put the salad on a platter, garnish with the hard-boiled egg slices or quarters, celery tops, or curly parsley.

Yields 4-6 servings.

CHICKEN PIE

Take two full-grown chickens (or more if they are small), disjoint them, and cut the backbone, &c., as small as convenient. Boil them with a few slices of salt pork, in water enough to cover them; let them boil quite tender; then take out the breast bone. After they boil and the scum is taken off, put in a little onion, cut very fine, not enough to taste distinctly, but just enough to flavor a little; rub some parsley very fine when dry, or cut fine when green; this gives pleasant flavor. Season well with salt and pepper, and add a few ounces of good fresh butter. When all is cooked well, have liquid enough to cover the chicken; then beat up two eggs and stir, also some sweet cream.

From *Mrs. Winslow's Domestic Receipt Book for 1868*

...Have ready a baking dish, lined, on the sides, with a light paste...put the pieces of chicken into this dish...pour over it the liquor from the stew-pan, cover with the light paste, ornamenting the cover with leaves cut from the paste, and bake forty-five minutes.

From *The Practical Cookbook,* by Mrs. Bliss, 1850

NINETEENTH-CENTURY CHICKEN pies vary quite a bit in complexity. For the filling, some sources say to prepare the chicken as for a fricassee; others merely have you fix boiled chicken with a flour-thickened gravy. The simplest fillings are pieces of cooked chicken with some flour sprinkled on and broth poured over. Crusts vary from biscuit-like crusts top and bottom, or just top, to pastry made with lard or drippings, either top and/or bottom or just top.

Mrs. Winslow's filling is a simplified white fricassee. Fortunately, you will be able to buy your chicken already cut up, and even boned, if you wish. Chickens are now bred to be fat, so added fat in the old recipe is superfluous.

Since chicken pie was part of Thanksgiving dinner in the 1800s, Mrs. Bliss's suggestion to ornament the top with leaves would create a very festive-looking dish. Any plain pastry recipe you like would be suitable for this.

This is an excellent dish to bake in the bake-kettle down hearth if you aren't planning to heat the oven. Preheat the kettle, set the pie inside, put on the lid and heap fresh coals on top. Check after ten minutes to make sure the top crust isn't scorching. Refresh the coals as needed. It will bake in 20-25 minutes.

CHICKEN PIE

Pie dough sufficient for a nine inch, two-crust pie
1 stewing chicken, cut up
1 medium onion
1 egg
1/2 cup cream
Chopped parsley to taste
Salt and pepper

Stew the chicken pieces in barely enough water to cover, with the onion chopped up and added. When the chicken is cooked, remove it from the pan, take the meat off the bones, about four cups worth, and keep it warm while you prepare the sauce.

Beat the egg well and mix into the cream. Add egg and cream mixture to about 1-1/2 cups broth, enough to cover the chicken in the pie plate, whisking and cooking until thickened slightly. Add parsley, salt and pepper.

Preheat oven to 425°. Line a deep 9-inch pie plate with half of the pie dough. Roll out the second and set aside. Reserve enough pastry from the scraps to make leaves for the top.

Put the chicken into the pie plate, pour the sauce over it, and cover with the top crust. Attach the leaves by moistening the undersides with a bit of water and laying them on the surface. Glaze with beaten egg white, if you wish.

Bake the pie at 425° for ten minutes, then reduce the oven to 350° and bake for an additional 30 minutes, or until the crust is golden.

Serves six.

ROAST TURKEY

212. Roast Turkey.

Let the turkey be picked clean, and washed and wiped dry inside and out. Have your stuffing, No. 2, prepared, fill the crop and then the body full, sew it up, put it on a spit, and roast it, before a moderate fire, three hours. If more convenient, it is equally good when baked.

From *New England Economical Housekeeper,* by Mrs. E.A. Howland, 1845

...fasten it to a spit; dredge it with flour; if the turkey is not very fat, put small bits of butter on the breast; if it is fat, no butter will be requisite; place it before a slow fire and turn it frequently until all the flour begins to brown; baste it continually with salt and water from the dripping-pan, and when half done dredge it again with flour. If the breast is browning too fast, put a piece of paper over it. Fifteen minutes before you wish to serve it, drip a little melted butter over it, from the basting spoon; dredge it with flour, let it brown,—and the turkey is roasted.

From *The Practical Cookbook,* by Mrs. Bliss, 1864

MOST PEOPLE WILL PREFER to use a stove oven for roasting turkey, but if you think you would enjoy trying to roast a turkey in your fireplace, and if you have a tin kitchen at your disposal, the instructions above will serve you well. Roasting times for a turkey, which averaged three hours for a ten-pound turkey stuffed, seem underdone according to modern preferences; you will want to cook your turkey longer than these instructions specify—four to five hours for an eight- to twelve-pound stuffed turkey, and longer for larger birds.

Stuffing recipes follow.

Depending on your skill in the fireplace, it need not take longer than it would in a standard oven at 325°, and you can tell if the bird is done by pricking it with a fork at a joint to see if the juice runs clear, or by wiggling the drumstick up and down. It will move freely when the turkey is done. Double-check by using an instant-read thermometer aiming for a temperature of 185°.

See the roast chicken instructions (page 63) for further advice on roasting poultry, and for gravy directions.

BOILED TURKEY

The turkey should be prepared as for roasting, with the wings twisted over the back. Stuff the turkey as follows: Pour boiling water on wheat bread or mashed potatoes; season high with pepper and salt, and if liked, a teaspoonful of sage or thyme, or a bunch of fine chopped parsley; fill the crop, and turn the skin of the neck over against the back and fasten with a small skewer.

Dredge with flour over the outside; tie it in a cloth, and put it in a pot of hot (not boiling) water; cover the pot, and let it boil gently about fifteen minutes to the pound; take off the skum; serve with drawn butter, celery or parsley sauce.

From *Practical American Cookery and Domestic Economy*, by Miss Hall, 1855

BOILING TURKEYS AND CHICKENS was common in the nineteenth century and offered the advantages of preventing the bird from being dried out as it sometimes is in roasting and requiring less assiduous tending. Stuff the turkey with your choice of stuffings. Enclose the turkey in a muslin cloth, basted shut.

If you are game to try this method, allow 20 minutes to the pound.

In addition to the sauces suggested above, oyster sauce was another accompaniment to boiled turkey; an oyster-sauce recipe is found on page 71.

In a fireplace, you will need a sizeable kettle to hold the turkey, and a well-maintained mature fire, which will keep the bird at a steady simmer. Have a tea-kettle of hot water at hand to add as the cooking water evaporates.

BASIC STUFFING

211. Stuffing, No. 2

Take dry pieces of bread or crackers, chop them fine, put in small pieces of butter or a little cream, with sage, pepper and salt, one egg, and a small quantity of flour, moistened with milk.

From *New England Economical Housekeeper,* by Mrs. E.A. Howland, 1845

POUNDED CRACKERS and bread crumbs were used interchangeably in nineteenth-century stuffing recipes. Sometimes salt pork or sausage was included. From time to time lemon and such spices as cinnamon and nutmeg were added. This recipe gives you a very basic stuffing that you can elaborate upon as you wish.

The rule of thumb for stuffing is to provide one cup of stuffing for each pound of bird. If your crumbs are very dry, you will need to add some water or milk, but only enough to moisten them. If you use an egg, plan on one for every three to four cups of crumbs. The seasoning must be done to your taste, but start with sage, salt and pepper.

1-1/2 slices of bread for one cup of crumbs
2 tablespoons melted butter per cup of crumbs, (less if you add sausage or salt pork)
1/4 teaspoon dried rubbed sage
Onion and celery chopped
Salt and pepper
Hot water

Empty the crumbs into a large mixing bowl, and drizzle in the melted butter, add the seasonings and toss, sprinkling in hot water until the crumbs are evenly moist. Pack loosely into the turkey or chicken's cavity. Close up using skewers or sewing it shut with heavy thread.

OYSTER SAUCE

12 oysters, cut into thirds
1 cupful of milk
2 tablespoonfuls of butter
2 teaspoonfuls rice or wheat flour
Flavoring to taste
Chopped parsley

Drain the liquor from the oysters before you cut them up. Boil the liquor two min-
utes, and add the milk. When this is scalding hot, strain and return to the
saucepan. Wet the flour with cold water and stir into the sauce. As it thickens, put
in the butter, then pepper and salt, with a very little parsley. The juice of half a
lemon is pleasant flavoring. Stir it in after taking the sauce from the fire. Before
this, and as soon as the flour is well incorporated with the other ingredients, add
the oysters, each cut into three pieces. Simmer five minutes and pour into the gravy
tureen. Some also pour a little over the turkey on the dish. Garnish with slices of
boiled egg and celery tops.

From *The Dinner Year Book,* by Marion Harland, 1878

A dozen oysters, coarsely chopped
2 tablespoons of butter
1 tablespoon of flour
1 cup of milk
Juice of half a lemon (optional)
Parsley
Salt and pepper

Drain the oysters, reserving the liquor. Melt the butter in a heavy saucepan, whisk in the flour and cook for a minute or two until it bubbles. Add the oyster liquor, whisking to prevent lumps, and then add the milk. Bring just to a boil then reduce the temperature. Cook for two minutes. Add the oysters, and simmer gently for 2 to 5 minutes. Add the lemon juice, parsley, salt and pepper. Taste and adjust seasonings.

Serve in a gravy or sauce boat.

Yields about 2 cups.

GRAVY SAUCE FOR BOILED FOWLS

Gravy Sauce

Boil the neck, wing, gizzard, liver, and heart of the fowls, till they are tender; put in a boiled onion, chop it all up fine, then add two or three pounded crackers, a piece of butter, and a little flour thickening; season it with pepper and salt.

From *New England Economical Housekeeper,* by Mrs. E.A. Howland, 1845

THIS IS SIMILAR TO the giblet gravy we make today, though people seldom thicken anything with pounded crackers. How closely you wish to follow the original is up to you. Most of us leave the wings on the bird, and would be unhappy at finding bits of neck bones in our gravy, if that is really what Mrs. Howland meant. Since this was for boiled fowls, there were no pan juices to use. I have added seasonings to this sauce to enhance the flavor.

GIBLET GRAVY

Neck, gizzard, liver, and heart of turkey or chicken
3 cups of water or more if needed to cover giblets
1 onion
1 stalk of celery, cut up
1 carrot cut up
1 bay leaf
1/2 teaspoon thyme
Salt and pepper

Put the neck, gizzard, liver, and heart, and the onion and seasonings, in a saucepan with the water to boil together until all are well cooked. You can use this liquid for basting the roasting fowl, being sure to add water as necessary so it does not cook dry and so that you'll have 2-1/2 to 3 cups of broth. Just before the fowl is done cooking, remove the giblets and vegetables with a slotted spoon, and chop all finely and set aside. Reserve the broth. Then proceed to the instructions for boiled or roasted fowls which follow.

To make a sauce or gravy down hearth, you will need a trivet with a heavy bottom pan, or a skillet with legs. Keep your coal shovel right at hand to add or remove coals as needed.

FOR BOILED FOWLS

2 cups of broth from giblets
2 tablespoon butter
2 common crackers or 1/4 cup of
    pounded crackers or
2 tablespoons flour whisked or
    shaken in 1/3 cup water
Salt and pepper

Put the broth into a heavy saucepan, add the butter, and stir it all together. Then add the thickening of your choice (crackers or flour), cook and stir to avoid sticking or lumps. Taste and adjust seasoning, and then if you wish, add chopped giblets and/or vegetables. Bring to a simmer, and serve in a gravy boat. This recipe is easily doubled if you need more sauce.

Yield is two cups minimum but varies, depending on the amount of the giblets.

FOR ROASTED FOWLS

2 cups of broth from giblets
2 tablespoons flour shaken in
    1/3 cup water
Salt and pepper

When you take the fowl from the oven, put it on a platter and cover to keep it warm. Put the broth into the roasting pan, and put it over a medium heat, stirring the pan gravy to loosen the stuck on bits. Pour all the resulting liquid into a measuring cup. Put two tablespoons of fat into the roasting pan, and whisk in two tablespoons of flour, cooking for a couple of minutes until the flour is bubbling. Add the broth whisking steadily to avoid lumps, and cook until the gravy is thick and smooth. If needed, add a little more broth to get the consistency you wish.

Taste and adjust seasoning then add the chopped giblets, and bring to a simmer.

This recipe is easily increased: For every cup of broth, put one tablespoon of fat back into the roasting pan, together with one tablespoon of flour.

Yield is two cups minimum but varies, depending on the amount of the giblets.

STUFFING FOR ROASTED GOOSE OR DUCK

To Roast a Goose.—Goose in itself is of a strong rich flavor, and requires both nicety in the cooking as well as in the stuffing .... There are many modes of stuffing: for one mode take two moderate sized onions, and boil them rapidly ten minutes; then chop them finely; mince sage to the quantity of half the onion; add of powdered bread twice as much as onion; pepper and salt in it; introduce a little cayenne, and then bind it with the beaten yolk of an egg. Potatoes mashed are sometimes introduced, but not frequently, into the body. They should be mashed with floury potatoes mixed with a little cream and a little fresh butter rather highly seasoned with cayenne and salt. Both ends of the goose should be secured, when trussed, that the seasoning may not escape. It should be roasted before a quick fire, and kept constantly basted. A piece of white paper may be placed over the breast, while roasting, until it rises, and then it may be removed. It will take from an hour an a half to an hour and three quarters...

Boil some sage and some onions, and some apples; chop all fine together; a little pepper and salt, a little mustard, juice of lemon, a few bread crumbs; bind all together with a little good stock, or milk, or butter; ...

From *"Receipts &c.," Godey's Lady's Book,* 1857

GODEY'S CONCENTRATED on the stuffing, assuming a cooks familiarity with roasting process. Goose and duck are fatty meats, and even modern recipes recommend onions or apples in the stuffing and serving apple, onion, or a "sharp" sauce to help cut the oiliness. For advice on roasting ducks and geese (see page 77).

ONION AND SAGE STUFFING

2 large onions
1 tablespoon olive oil or butter
4 cups bread crumbs (about 6 slices
    of bread)
Handful of fresh sage or
    1-1/2 tablespoons dried
Salt and pepper
1/4 teaspoon cayenne
1 egg yolk, beaten

Chop onions coarsely and sauté in the butter or olive oil over a medium heat for three to five minutes or until they just begin to soften. Remove from the heat and toss together with crumbs and sage to mix well. Add the seasonings to taste and then stir in the beaten yolk.

Stuff loosely into the goose, and proceed with the roasting instructions on page 77.

Yields 3-4 cups stuffing.

APPLE AND ONION STUFFING

2 cups quartered apples
2 large onions, chopped coarsely
Handful of fresh sage or
** 2 teaspoons dried**
1 cup dried bread crumbs
Salt and pepper
1 teaspoon ground mustard
Juice of 1 lemon
Broth or milk

Put the apples and onions to a heavy sauce pan with only enough water to cover the bottom of the pan. Cover and stew them about ten minutes. Then remove from the heat and chop them together. Toss the chopped apples and onions together with the sage, crumbs, salt and pepper, mustard, and lemon juice to mix well. Add enough broth or milk to bind loosely.

Stuff into the goose and proceed with the instructions for roasting on page 77.

Yields 1-1/2 cups stuffing.

POTATO STUFFING

1 medium onion
1 tablespoon dried sage or three
** or four fresh leaves**
2 cups hot mashed potatoes
1 tablespoon vinegar
1/8 to 1/4 teaspoon cayenne
** pepper to taste**
Salt and pepper to taste

If you are using fresh sage, chop the sage and onion together. Otherwise, add the dried sage to the potato and mix it with vinegar, cayenne, salt, and pepper, blending well. Taste and adjust seasonings.

Stuff loosely into the goose or duck, leaving a little space in the opening, and proceed with the instructions for roasting on page 77.

Yields about two cups of stuffing, sufficient for 6 pounds of goose or duck.

SHARP SAUCE FOR GOOSE

Previous to sending [a roasted goose] to table, a flavoring may be made as follows: To a dessert-spoonful of made mustard, add a quarter of a teaspoonful of cayenne pepper, about the same quantity of salt; mix it evenly with a glass of port wine and two glasses of rich gravy; make it hot; cut a slit in the apron of the goose, and pour it through just previously to serving.

From *Godey's Lady's Book,* 1855

THIS SNAPPY SAUCE would help cut the fattiness of a roasted goose or duck. A mild Dijon mustard or similar mild mustard is very good in this recipe. Add the cayenne gradually, tasting as you go to make sure it is not overwhelming the flavor of the sauce. This sauce has to be prepared after the gravy has been made. For gravy instructions see page 72, substituting goose or duck giblets for the chicken or turkey giblets.

SHARP SAUCE FOR GOOSE OR DUCK

1/2 cup of gravy made from goose or duck drippings
2 tablespoons Dijon-style prepared mustard
1/8 to 1/4 teaspoon cayenne pepper
1/4 teaspoon salt
1/4 cup port

Whisk all the ingredients together. Heat until it bubbles. Taste and adjust seasonings. Serve it separately in a gravy boat.

Yields about 3/4 cup sauce.

ROASTED GOOSE OR DUCK

214. To roast Geese and Ducks.

Boiling water should be poured all over, and inside, of a goose or duck before you prepare them for cooking, to take out the strong oily taste. Let the fowl be picked clean, and wiped dry with a cloth, inside and out: fill the body and crop with stuffing, No. 1 or 2. If you prefer not to stuff it, put an onion inside; put it down to the fire, and roast it brown. It will take about two hours and a half.

From *New England Economical Housekeeper,* by Mrs. E.A. Howland, 1845

THE GENERAL RULE today for ducks and geese is 30 minutes per pound. You may use any of the stuffings suggested for roasted goose on pages 74 and 75, or Mrs. Howland's Stuffing #2, on page 70. Or you may wish merely to put an onion in the duck instead of stuffing.

Modern cookbooks caution against basting a goose or duck as it roasts. It is a good idea to place the bird on a rack so the fat can run freely and, in fact, you may want to prick it in several places as it cooks to allow the fat under the skin to run off.

If you plan to roast a duck or goose in the fireplace, follow the general roasting instructions on page 63. Practice poultry roasting on a chicken or turkey before trying ducks and geese. Be prepared for a lot of fat to run out, spatter, and cook onto the dripping pan. You may wish to empty the dripping pan partway through the process.

Preheat oven to 325°. Remove as much of the visible fat from the duck as you can and prepare for roasting as you would a turkey. Most of the stuffing recipes on pages 74-75 will yield enough for a duck, but you may need to increase the recipe for a goose weighing between 10 and 12 pounds to about 3 cups of stuffing. Put 2 to 4 cups stuffing into the bird loosely, truss, and place on a rack in a pan. Roast allowing half an hour to a pound, pricking occasionally, and basting only if it appears to be drying out.

At the end of the cooking time, remove from oven and allow to continue draining fat while you make a gravy which you can do by draining some of the fat from the drippings and proceeding as you would for the gravy on page 72.

PORK CHOPS WITH TOMATO GRAVY

Pork Chops, With Tomato Gravy.

Trim off skin and fat; rub all over with a mixture of powdered sage and onion. Put a small piece of butter into a frying pan; put in the chops, and cook rather slowly, as they should be well done. Lay the chops upon a hot dish; add a little hot water to the gravy in the pan; a great spoonful of butter rolled in flour, pepper, salt, and sugar, and a half a cup of juice drained from a can of tomatoes——keeping the tomatoes for a tomato for a tomato omelette [sic] for breakfast. Stew five minutes and pour over the chops.

From *The Dinner Year Book* by Marion Harland [Mary Virginia Terhune] 1878

AFTER SLOWLY ADOPTING tomatoes starting in the late 1700s, New Englanders enjoyed eating them by the last half of the 1800s, often growing them in home gardens and canning them at home, and buying locally canned tomatoes, too. Even the Mystic area had a small cannery that put up locally grown tomatoes.

Modern pork chops come with their skin already trimmed off, and often only a narrow band of fat still attached. And because Marion Harland provided in her *Dinner Year Book,* a main meal menu for every day, she often refers to other meals as she uses up leftovers from one or sets up leftovers for another, as she did here. I recommend planning to serve stewed tomatoes with your pork chops, and reserve some of the liquid for the tomato gravy.

1 small onion minced
1/2 teaspoon sage
4 pork chops
1 tablespoon of butter or olive oil
   plus one tablespoon of butter
1/4 cup of boiling water
1 tablespoon of flour
Salt and pepper
2 teaspoons of sugar
1/2 cup of reserved tomato liquid
   or tomato juice

Toss together the minced onion and the dried sage, and press it onto the surface of the pork chops. Heat a heavy frying pan and put one tablespoon of butter or olive oil into it and heat it until a drop of water will jump. Put the pork chops in the pan, and reduce the heat and cover. Cook the chops for about ten minutes a side. Remove them and put them on a plate and keep them warm while you prepare the gravy. Add the boiling water to the fry pan and cook, scraping up bits of browned drippings in the pan. Mash the butter, the flour, salt, pepper, and sugar together, and add it to the pan, whisking to prevent lumps, and then add the tomato liquid or juice. Cook together until slightly reduced and somewhat thickened, taste and adjust seasoning. If you wish, return the chops to the fry pan and re-warm them. Serve them on the platter with the gravy poured over it.

Serves four.

5 Seafood

TODAY NEW ENGLAND IS FAMOUS FOR ITS SEAFOOD. In the nineteenth-century, the region's favorites included cod, haddock, salt cod, salmon, mackerel, shad, lobsters, and oysters, and as the century wore on, halibut, freshly caught sport fish like bluefish, trout, and bass. Clams began their career as the favored bait for codfish, but by the end of the century won favor fried, in clam chowder, fritters, and at clambakes.

Few early recipes fail to add butter, eggs, or salt pork to the fish. To modern people whose interest is in lower calorie fare, fish is naturally a good choice, the added fat is puzzling. But for nineteenth-century Yankees who worked hard, walked or rode horseback everywhere, and lived in cold houses, fish simply never packed the caloric punch they wanted and needed. The sauces compensated giving fish dishes substance.

Fireplace cooks will find many of these recipes easy to use down-hearth. More specific instructions accompany the appropriate recipes.

BAKED BLUEFISH

Score the fish down the back, and lay in a dripping pan. Pour over it a cup of hot water in which have been melted two tablespoonfuls of butter. Bake one hour, basting every ten minutes; twice with butter, twice with the gravy, and again twice with butter. Take up the fish and keep hot, while you strain the gravy into a saucepan; thicken with flour; add a teaspoonful of anchovy paste, the juice of half a lemon with a little of the grated peel, pepper and salt. Boil up, pour half over the fish, the rest into a boat. Garnish the fish with eggs, quartered lengthwise, lettuce hearts, and quartered lemons.

From *The Dinner Year Book* by Marion Harland, 1878

BLUEFISH IS A ROBUST, delicious, oily fish at its best only hours out of the ocean and since it is considered an excellent sport fish, you may be lucky enough to have a fisherman friend who will deliver up a fine whole blue straight from the boat.

A whole three-to-four-pound blue will bake as above in 30 to 40 minutes and serve four to six people. You can test for doneness by seeing whether the flesh flakes apart and the juice runs clear. You can baste the fish with the pan juices and/or brush it with additional butter or olive oil, or a mixture of the two.

THE FISH

One 3-4 pound bluefish, in the round
Salt and pepper
A bundle of herbs (parsley, tarragon,
**   scallions, dill)**
1 cup hot water with one tablespoon
**   of butter or olive oil in it**
2-3 tablespoons of melted butter
**   or olive oil**

SAUCE

Pan juices
Flour
1 teaspoon of anchovy paste
Juice of one-half lemon
Grated or shredded peel of one-half lemon
Quartered lemons
Hardboiled eggs, quartered (optional)

Preheat the oven to 350°. Wash the fish inside and out, and lay it on a piece of cheesecloth doubled over in your baking pan. Open it, salt and pepper the interior, and stuff in the bundle of herbs. Pour the hot water and butter over the fish. Bake for about 15 minutes per pound of fish, or until the fish flakes apart in the thickest section. Every 10 to 15 minutes baste it with the pan juices, or brush it with the butter or olive oil. When the fish is done, lift it with the cheesecloth and slide it onto the serving dish. Cover it with foil and set aside while you make the sauce.

Turn the sauce out into a measuring cup. For every 1 cup of pan juice, allow 2 tablespoons of flour. Return a small mount of the pan gravy to the baking pan, and whisk in the flour, gradually adding more pan juice, whisking constantly to avoid lumps, and put over a medium heat to cook. Keep whisking, and add the anchovy paste, lemon juice, and peel. Cook until the sauce is smooth and thick; taste and adjust seasonings. Serve sauce in a separate pitcher.

Unwrap the fish, garnish with shredded lettuce and lemon wedges, and if you wish, quartered eggs.

Serves four to six.

BACALHAU

Flake apart salt codfish which has been soaked overnight and cooked. Get all the bones out. Cook lots of onions—3-4—with a little olive oil, garlic, paprika, salt and pepper, the onions fried till soft only. Put the fish on a plate with boiled and quartered potatoes around, and spread the onions on top, garnish with hard cooked eggs, and chickpeas.

From *Rose Camacho Hirsch*, Stonington, Connecticut, 1988

ROSE HIRSCH'S MOTHER, Maria Goulart Camacho of Stonington, Connecticut prepared salt codfish this way at Christmastime, as many families still do. Follow the preceding instructions for soaking salt codfish.

3-4 medium potatoes
1 pound salt cod, soaked boned,
   and cooked
1 tablespoon olive oil
3 large onions
3 cloves of garlic
1 teaspoon paprika (or more to taste)
Salt and pepper
2 hard boiled eggs cut into wedges
1/2 cup cooked garbanzos

Put the potatoes on to boil. Lay the salt cod in a pan covered with cold water and bring to a simmer. Cook it until the fish flakes apart. Take the fish off the heat, drain it, and as soon as you can handle it, flake it apart, removing all bones. Set aside but keep the flaked fish hot. Put the olive oil in a heavy frying pan, and cook the onions and garlic 8 to 10 minutes or until soft and golden. Stir in the paprika, salt, and pepper. Drain the potatoes. Lay the fish on a platter, surround it with the potatoes, spread the fried onions on top, and garnish with the eggs and garbanzos.

Yields 4-6 servings.

BOILED SALT COD, OR DUN FISH

Put a salt cod, weighing seven or eight pounds into a sufficient quantity of water to cover it, and let it stand in a warm place overnight. In the morning pour off this water, wash the fish clean, put it into a kettle with cold water, add enough to cover it, and place the kettle where the water will scald. Keep the water scalding hot until within half an hour of dinner; turn off this hot water, and replace it with cold water, let it have one boil up, and the fish is ready for the table....

Pork scraps are made as follows.—Cut two slices of salt fat pork into very small bits, put these bits into a frying-pan and over a hot fire; stir them frequently until all the fat is extracted and they are a light brown crisp; serve in a sauce tureen.

From *The Practical Cookbook*, by Mrs. Bliss, 1864

MOST NEW ENGLANDERS like their boiled salt cod dinner served up with boiled vegetables such as potatoes, beets, and carrots, just as they enjoyed with their boiled corned beef dinner. Fried salt-pork scraps or an egg sauce were popular accompaniments. Because the salt fish is soaked and scalded, most salt is removed so the pork fat and scraps do not make the dish overpoweringly salty. In fact, they add needed flavor.

Salt cod is very expensive today, and whole fish are virtually impossible to find. One pound of salt cod will serve four, possibly with some leftovers for codfish cakes or breakfast hash. Modern salt cod is salted but not completely desiccated, so once it is soaked, 20 minutes of a gentle simmer will make it tender enough to flake apart.

Mrs. Bliss, above refers to "dun" fish, a very old designation for the best quality of salted fish, so called because in the curing it became a yellow-brown, dun, color.

1 pound of salt cod
4-6 carrots
4-6 small beets
4-5 medium potatoes

Soak the fish 6-8 hours in fresh cold water. Start boiling the vegetables about 30 minutes before you begin the fish; you may wish to boil the beets separately from the carrots and potatoes. Drain the fish and lay it in a pan. Cover it with fresh water and bring it to a simmer but do not allow to boil. Cook until it flakes apart, about 15 to 20 minutes. Serve fish and vegetables together on a platter with a sauce of your choice.

Egg sauce is found on page 93. For fried salt pork, cut two slices off a half pound piece of lean salt pork. Cut into small cubes less than a half inch square. Fry until they are golden, and drain them. If you wish, drizzle the fat over the fish and vegetables and garnish with the scraps, or just sprinkle the fish with the scraps.

SALT FISH HASH

Salt fish mashed with potatoes, with good butter or pork scraps to moisten, is nicer the second day than it was the first. The fish should be minced very fine, while it is still warm. After it has got cold and dry it is difficult to do it nicely. Salt fish needs plenty of vegetables, such as onions, beets, carrots, etc.

From *The American Frugal Housewife*, by Mrs. Child, 1833

HASH IS WHAT YOU MADE out of your leftover boiled salt-codfish dinner. The proportion of vegetables to fish depended entirely on the leftovers and personal taste, so there can be no more specific a recipe than Mrs. Child has provided. If you include beets they will, of course, turn the whole thing red. It really does taste better with salt pork or real butter.

This is an excellent dish to cook in the fireplace, using a hanging griddle or a fry pan set on a low trivet.

BOILED SALT COD, PORTUGUESE STYLE

Soak, cook, and debone the salt codfish, and serve it with boiled potatoes and cooked kale or collards. Pour olive oil over it, and pepper it.

From *Rose Camacho Hirsch*, Stonington, Connecticut, 1988

PREPARE SALT COD this way for a lighter version of a salt cod dinner. Steam the kale or collards, or sauté lightly in olive oil with a little garlic or chopped onion. This dish calls for a well-flavored olive oil. Serve more oil on the table in a cruet so people can add more if they wish.

1 pound of salt cod

4 medium potatoes

One bunch (or four to five large leaves) of kale

Olive oil

Salt and pepper to taste

To prepare the fish, follow the steps specified on page 84 for the boiled salt cod dinner. Trim the kale, removing the tough center stalk, and coarsely chopping the leaves. Cook the potatoes separately, and ten minutes before serving time, steam or sauté the kale. Lay the fish and vegetables on a platter, and drizzle olive oil to taste over all. Finish with sea salt and a few grinds of pepper.

Serves four.

BACALHAU CON ARROZ

Soak, cook, and debone the salt codfish and flake into cooked rice. Add assafroa (safflower) and cumin.

From Rose Camacho Hirsch, Stonington, Connecticut, 1988

ANOTHER WAY TO PREPARE salt cod is to combine it with rice instead of potatoes, much as you would for kedgeree (see page 98). You can use leftover boiled salt cod in this dish (follow the instructions for boiled salt codfish on page 84) and the traditional Portuguese seasonings of safflower and cumin make this special. You can actually use any proportion of fish to rice you like though the following recipe recommends an equal proportion of rice to fish.

2 tablespoons of olive oil
1 medium onion chopped
1/2 cup cooked rice
1/2 cup cooked, boned, salt codfish
3/4 teaspoon ground cumin
1/4 teaspoon powdered safflower

Select a sauté pan large enough to hold all the ingredients. Sauté the onion in the olive oil, and when it is soft, after about five minutes, add all the rest of the ingredients and toss them together, and warm them through, putting a lid on the pan briefly if necessary.

Serves two.

PICKED-UP CODFISH

Pull the fish in little bits, then soak half an hour in a good deal of cold water. Pour off the water, put the fish in a saucepan, and add more cold water; simmer till tender. If too salt, pour off the water in which it is cooking, and again cover with cold water, and when it boils up drain off the water and cover with good thick cream, and add a piece of butter half the size of an egg, or larger if the cream is not rich. Set over the stove til it boils up, and thicken with flour wet with water. Stir in a beaten egg while hot, and serve.

From *All Around the House*, by Mrs. H.W. Beecher, 1878

THIS DISH IS SO SIMILAR to the salt pork and salt beef gravies (pages 54 and 59) that you can simply substitute the salted codfish for the meat. Using cream and adding an egg as Mrs. Beecher suggests makes this a richer dish. In southeastern Connecticut and Rhode Island, codfish gravy or creamed codfish was and is frequently served on jonnycakes. Elsewhere it was served over potatoes or toast.

The trick to this dish is in shredding or "picking-up" the fish *before* soaking it.

1/2 pound of salt cod
1 cup of milk or cream
2 tablespoons of butter
2 tablespoons of flour or 1 egg

Shred the salt cod with two forks or your fingers. Put it into the pan you intend to cook it in; cover with fresh cold water and let soak for half an hour. Drain, and recover with fresh water and put over a medium heat until it simmers, taste, and if it is still too salty for your taste, drain it, and repeat.

When it comes to a simmer again, drain it, and add the cream to the fish, plus the butter, and bring again to a simmer. If the sauce seems too thin, dredge the flour over it while stirring it gently until the flour is incorporated. If you prefer to use the egg, beat it in a separate bowl with some of the hot cream spooned from the pan and then add the beaten egg to the fish, stirring until it is well mixed.

Serve this for supper or lunch over jonnycakes, (page 44), baked or boiled potatoes, toasted bread or crackers.

Yields 4-6 servings.

CODFISH CAKES

Soak codfish overnight, and scald it, add to it twice its quantity of boiled potatoes, knead all well together, make in small cakes and fry in butter. If, after having boiled cod fish, you have some left, use it in the same way. It makes a nice and wholesome dish.

From *The Complete Domestic Guide*, by Mrs. L.G. Abell, 1853

ANOTHER LEFTOVER DISH, usually eaten at breakfast and known variously as fish cakes or fish balls, was usually made out of salt cod. In 1833, Mrs. Child wrote that "There is no way of preparing salt fish for breakfast, so nice as to roll it up in little balls, after it is mixed with mashed potatoes; dip it into an egg, and fry it brown."

This New England classic would also work as an appetizer, and is an easy dish for fireplace cookery. In fact, if you are having a group of people over for your hearth cooked meal, fry these up in your hanging griddle or on a fry pan over a low trivet, and present them hot with a dab of ketchup or salsa as the appetizer straight from the fire. If you are making the fish cakes from scratch, from salt cod, follow the instructions for boiling salt cod (page 84). Then follow the following instructions.

1 cup cooked salt cod
2 cups boiled potatoes
Butter or bacon drippings

With a fork, finely shred the boiled cod. Mash the potatoes very smooth in a separate pan (adding, if you wish, butter, pepper, and a little milk). Blend the fish and potatoes. Shape the fishcakes into the desired size and fry till golden brown on both sides.

Yields 6-8 three-inch by 1/2-inch thick fishcakes or 28 two-inch diameter appetizer-sized fish cakes.

STEWED HADDOCK

To make stewed haddock, poach the fish lightly first, then stew it in a mixture of butter, salt, pepper, and cream. Serve over "cream lunch biscuits."

From Frances Jaixen Dodge, Block Island, Rhode Island, May 1986

IN 1986 MRS. DODGE described to me this way of preparing stewed haddock as she remembered it being prepared when she was a girl. She surmised that her father might have cooked haddock this way when he was the Block Island Life Saving Service cook in the mid-1900s. This is a nice dish for winter supper and is ideal for people who prefer a mild-flavored fish.

1 pound of filleted haddock
Salted water to cover
1 cup of cream
Butter
Salt and pepper to taste
Cream Lunch biscuits or toast

Put the fish into a heavy pan. Salt the water until it tastes briny and add enough of it to cover the fish. Bring to a simmer until the haddock is just cooked through, about 10 to 15 minutes, depending on the thickness of the fish. Drain the fish, and add cream, butter, salt, and pepper—all to taste—and re-warm over moderate heat. Serve over cream lunch biscuits, which will soak up the cream. You can also use pilot crackers, saltines, or toast.

Serves two to three.

FRIED HALIBUT STEAKS

Wash and wipe the steaks. Roll each in flour, and fry upon a buttered griddle, turning carefully with a spatula, or cake-turner, when the lower side is done. They should be of a nice brown, and tender throughout. Remove to a hot dish and garnish with sliced lemon; in carving see that a bit of the lemon goes to each person, as many prefer it to any other sauce for fish. Send around potatoes with the steak. Worcestershire is a good store-sauce for fish and game. Anchovy is preeminently a fish sauce, but many do not like it.

From *The Dinner Year Book*, by Marion Harland, 1878

SO SIMPLE, SO GOOD! Halibut are large, though not as large as they were in the 1800s, and the steaks can be substantial cuts depending on from where in the fish they are taken; hence Mrs. Harland's comment on "carving." The steaks hold together well if you don't remove the skin. These instructions work well with salmon steaks, too.

One-half a pound per person, cut in inch- to inch-and-a-half-thick slices
Flour seasoned with salt and pepper
Butter or olive oil
Worcestershire sauce

Toss together the flour, salt and pepper and put it onto a plate. Grease a heavy pan lightly with butter or olive oil, and have it hot. Lay the steak in the flour mixture on both sides and shake off the excess. Place on the hot pan, and then reduce the heat to medium, and fry them on each side about four to five minutes. When they are done, serve on a platter with wedges of lemon, and a dash of Worcestershire if you wish.

FISH GRILLED ON A GRIDIRON

TO BROIL SHAD, MACKEREL, AND SALMON.

Have the bars of the gridiron well greased with lard; lay your fish on, flesh side down; when half done, turn it and finish, skin down; when done, pour over sweet cream, if you have it, or spread over a little butter.

From *New England Economical Housekeeper*, by Mrs. E.A. Howland, 1845

THESE ARE CLEARLY instructions for broiling in a fireplace with bottom heat, a process today called grilling. I have always found broiling fish on gridirons over coals a bit tricky, no matter how carefully I proceeded. If you own a grilling device that clasps shut so that you can turn the fish at will without prying it off the bars of a gridiron, you may prefer to use that. Most of us buy fish already filleted, but for grilling try to get fish with skin on one side.

Establish a deep bed of ashes on one side of the fire, and lay a bed of coals on it as large in diameter as the fish to be broiled. Grease the bars of your gridiron and lay the fish on it, skin side down. When the fish begins to firm up, turn it. Take the gridiron off the coals, and freshen the coals as needed. Using a spatula or long knife, loosen the fish from the gridiron, place a plate over the fish, and, lifting the gridiron, flip the fish onto the plate. Replace the gridiron over the coals, then slide the fish from the plate to the gridiron again. When the fish is done, repeat this process to serve the fish skin-side down on a serving plate. Obviously, if it is a fish in the round then you will not have to do this last step.

Shad, mackerel, and salmon, oilier fish than many, are enhanced tremendously by being cooked over a wood fire or charcoal. These instructions are also perfectly useful for outdoor grilling.

Sweet cream *is* good poured over it, but you could get away with plain melted butter, or butter with chopped parsley or a squeeze of lemon juice. Plan on one-third to one-half pound of fish per person. Allow about 8 to 12 minutes per side, depending on the size of the fish.

POACHED SALMON

FRESH SALMON, BOILED

From the middle of a salmon weighing sixteen or eighteen pounds, take four pounds, wash it carefully, rub the inside with salt, tie it up in a cloth, and boil it slowly forty minutes; when half cooked turn it over in the pot, serve with egg sauce, or drawn butter and parsley.

From *The Practical Cookbook*, by Mrs. Bliss, 1864

IT IS EASIER TO POACH whole salmon than filleted, and it makes a handsome presentation. Buy a medium-sized salmon, preferably in the round, allowing at least half a pound per serving. Salmon steaks are also fairly easy to poach. Allow one steak per serving.

The modern rule of thumb for poaching fish is to allow 10 minutes per inch of thickness. Mrs. Bliss, above, wrapped her fish in a cloth which made it easy to handle and you may wish to do the same using cheese cloth. Alternatively, some fish poachers have slotted lifters inside them with handles that allow you to raise the fish out of the liquid. Sophisticated cooks may wish to use court bouillon (stock made from fish bones, heads, etc.) or white wine in a poaching liquid.

Serve with the egg sauce recipe that follows, either poured over the fish or served in a gravy boat on the side, and garnish the fish with additional boiled egg. If it is the Fourth of July, have fresh peas and new potatoes with it.

Salmon in the round
Salt
Water or court bouillon
An onion, a carrot, and a stalk or
   two of celery

Wrap the fish in cheese cloth and lay in a poacher or pan deep enough to allow it to be covered with liquid. Add enough salt to the liquid to make it taste quite briny, and pour it over the fish. Cut the vegetables up and add them to the poaching liquid, too. If you like cooking with herbs, feel free to add dill, tarragon, scallions, parsley, and a few sprigs of thyme.

Put over a medium heat and bring to a simmer, never allowing it to boil hard. Poach the fish about 10-12 minutes per inch of thickness or until it reaches an internal temperature of 140°.

When it is done, lift the fish from the liquid, lay on a platter, remove the cheese cloth, and delicately remove the skin before serving. Serve with egg sauce, or your favorite sauce.

EGG SAUCE

NO. 1 MELTED BUTTER

Melted Butter, sometimes called Drawn Butter, is made as follows: Braid two tea-spoonfuls of flour into a quarter of a pound of nice butter, stir this into four table-spoonfuls of boiling water, keep stirring until the butter is all melted; then let it boil up once, and it is fit for the tureen. If the butter and flour are not well braided, the sauce will be lumpy.

NO. 2 EGG SAUCE

Egg sauce is made by putting four hard-boiled eggs chopped fine, into the melted butter as above. A little more water is needed in the melted butter when egg sauce is to be made.

From *The Practical Cookbook*, by Mrs. Bliss, 1864

1/4 lb. or one stick of butter
2 teaspoons flour
1/2 cup hot water or fish stock
4 hard boiled eggs
Salt and pepper to taste

Rub the butter and flour together. In a heavy saucepan over a low heat, cook the mixture a few moments, then add a half cup of hot water or stock, and bring it up to a boil. Chop the eggs finely and add to the butter and flour mixture; add hot water or stock as needed to make the sauce a pouring consistency. Taste and adjust seasoning.

Yields 1-1/2 cups of sauce.

SALMON SALAD

Flake remnants of cold boiled salmon, mix with French, Mayonnaise, or Cream Dressing. Arrange on nests of lettuce leaves. Garnish with the yolk of a hard boiled egg forced through a potato ricer, and white of egg cut in strips.

From *The Boston Cooking-School Cookbook*, by Fannie Merritt Farmer, 1896

FOR MOST COLD OR SHELLFISH salads, Miss Farmer preferred French dressing, cream dressing, (see page 114), and mayonnaise, which is widely available. Salmon salad is a good way to use up leftover baked or poached salmon, and in a pinch you can substitute canned salmon. In the previous century and half, nearly all salads had eggs in them or used eggs for garnish, though many modern people will want to omit them.

You will want to use your favorite dressing, homemade or commercial, to assemble this salad. If you wish, you can add celery or scallions chopped finely to the salmon.

One way of garnishing was suggested in Marion Harland's *Dinner Year Book, 1878*, is accomplished by poking the yolks out of several slices of hard boiled eggs, and laying the rings around the salad. You can crumble the yolks into the salad, or sprinkle them on top. Mix this salad exactly as you would tuna salad.

BAKED SHAD

Put [the baked shad] into a hot dish, and keep warm while you add to the gravy a teaspoonful of anchovy sauce, the juice of a lemon, a tablespoonful of browned flour, wet up with cold water, and pepper. Boil up well, and serve in a boat.

From *The Dinner Year Book,* by Marion Harland, 1878

A WHOLE FRESH SHAD makes a magnificent dish, if there is a fisherman in your family to bring one home. You can bake a fillet with the pan covered so the juices from the fish do not evaporate, in which case you could make this sauce, which is very good and pleasantly lemony. Browned flour is not absolutely essential; make your own by running flour under the broiler briefly stirring it frequently until it has a rich golden color.

Pan juices from baked shad
1 teaspoon anchovy sauce
Juice of one-half lemon
1 tablespoon browned flour stirred
   with 2 tablespoons cold water
Pepper

Put the fish, stuffed with your favorite dressing, on a rack in a baking pan, and add 1/2- to 2/3-cup water. Bake at 350° till the fish flakes apart—about half an hour for a 3-4-pound whole fish.

Drain the pan juices into a heavy saucepan. Cover the fish with aluminum foil, and put into a warm oven while you make the sauce. Add the anchovy sauce, lemon juice, flour and water mixture, and pepper. Cook stirring constantly till thickened. To serve, put the fish on a platter, and pour the sauce over the fish or serve it in a gravy boat.

Yields about 2/3-cup gravy.

SCALLOPED ROES

The roes of the shad.
1 cup drawn butter, and the yolks of three hard-boiled eggs.
1 teaspoon anchovy paste.
Juice of half a lemon.
1 cup of bread crumbs.
Parsley, salt and pepper to taste.

Boil the roes in water with a little vinegar stirred in. Lay in cold water five minutes and wipe dry. Break up with the back of a spoon, but do not crush the eggs. Set by, and pound the boiled yolks to a powder. Beat this into the drawn butter, then the parsley and the other seasonings, finally the roes. Strew the bottom of a bake-dish with crumbs; pour in the mixture, and cover thickly with fine crumbs. Stick dots of butter over the top, and bake, covered, until it begins to bubble, then brown upon the upper grating of the oven.

From *The Dinner Year Book,* by Marion Harland, 1878

THIS IS A DELICIOUS WAY to prepare shad roe and a nice change from the fairly common roe and bacon combination. Since, by modern standards, nineteenth-century recipes are often heavy-handed with butter, I have reduced the amount of butter considerably. You may like to use a combination of olive oil and butter.

1-1/2 pounds or 3 roe sets
4 cups water with 3 tablespoons vinegar
mixed in
3 hard-boiled eggs
1/2 cup drawn butter
1 teaspoon anchovy paste
Parsley, salt, and pepper to taste
1 cup bread crumbs
Parmesan cheese (optional)

In a non-reactive pan poach the roes in the vinegar and water for about 5 minutes. Lay in cold water for 5 minutes, then drain and pat dry. Preheat oven to 350°. While the oven is heating, break the roes gently with the back of a spoon without crushing the eggs in the roe. Mash the egg yolks and beat into the drawn butter. Mix in parsley, salt, pepper, anchovy paste, and then the roes. Grease a 9-inch square baking pan and sprinkle the bread crumbs over the bottom. Spread the butter and roe mixture over the crumbs. Put dots of butter on the top, if you wish, or a sprinkle of Parmesan cheese. Bake covered for 15 minutes. When it begins to bubble, uncover and let brown under the broiler for another 2-3 minutes or until it is a nice golden color.

Yields 5-6 servings.

FRIED TROUT

Brook trout … must be split nearly to the tail to clean. Wash and drain. For a dozen good sized trout, fry six slices of salt pork; when brown, take out the pork, and put in the trout. Fry a nice brown on all sides. Serve the pork with them.

From *The Appledore Cook Book,* by Maria Parloa, 18xx

WHOLE SPLIT TROUT are wonderful cooked on the hearth, either fried as Maria Parloa suggests above or broiled on a gridiron. Cook them with the skin on in order to hold the fish together.

Allow one trout for each serving. You can buy whole, cleaned fish in many supermarket fish sections; otherwise, if you are cooking freshly caught trout, you will have to split and clean them yourself. You can also consider dredging the fish with cornmeal on both sides before frying them.

6 fresh trout
Pepper
6 thick slices of salt pork
   or bacon
2 medium onions, chopped

Wipe the trout inside and out, and lightly pepper the insides. Fry the salt pork or bacon in a large heavy pan, or plan to fry the fish in batches if your pan is not large enough to hold them all. When the pork or bacon is crisp, remove it and drain it on paper towels, and fry the fish in the fat in the pan for about two minutes per side. Put the fish on a plate and keep warm in the oven while you fry the onions in the same pan until they are soft. Crumble or chop finely the bacon or salt pork and strew it and the onions over the trout to serve.

Serves six.

KEDGEREE

Warm cold flaked fish slightly over hot water; and just before serving stir in one egg, beaten with one to two tablespoonfuls of hot milk and a bit of butter, and serve in a rice border. Steam the rice, one cupful, in two cupfuls of highly seasoned stock, in a double boiler, thirty minutes or until tender and dry.

From *The Boston Cook Book* by Mary Lincoln, 1913

MOST SOURCES AGREE that "kedgeree" is a corruption of the Hindi word "khichri," the name for a dish of lentils, or dal, onions, eggs, and condiments. In Europe and England, and then later in the United States, fish replaced the lentils. The dish was associated with breakfast but would make a snug supper. Nineteenth-century New Englanders were cautious about seasoning foods, but you don't have to be. This dish is enhanced with curry powder, a little red pepper, and onions. It is also a terrific way to serve leftover finnan haddie. Serve with chutney.

1/2 cup of milk
1 egg
1 cup cooked salt cod, finnan haddie, or fresh fish
Salt and pepper
1 tablespoonful butter (optional)
1 small onion chopped and sautéed (optional)
1 tablespoon curry powder (optional)
1 teaspoon red pepper flakes (optional)
2 cups of cooked rice

Whisk together the milk and the egg and put into the top of a double boiler, or into a heavy bottomed sauce pan.

Heat the mixture gradually until it thickens slightly, then add the fish, stirring to coat the fish, and heat it all through. Add salt and pepper to taste and a tablespoon of butter if you wish. Add any of the optional ingredients; taste and adjust seasonings. Serve over rice.

Serves 2-3.

FINNAN HADDIE

Smoking haddock was, according to tradition, developed in Findon, Scotland, and "Finnan haddie" is a corruption of "Findon Haddie" or Findon-style haddock. It came to New England along with an influx of fishermen from the Scottish influenced Canadian maritime provinces in the later 1800s and early 1900s, though earlier Americans also smoked fish, particularly oilier fishes like herring.

Take a wee taste of the fish before you decide whether you will soak it in cold water before cooking it. Modern finnan haddie is often not as salty as in the past, and will be partly cooked by the smoking process. Simmering finnan haddie in milk was and is the simplest way to prepare it for eating. It can be served for lunch, brunch, or supper, or even as an appetizer for a dinner. Put the pieces of fish on toast or boiled or baked potatoes and spoon the milk on as a sauce.

Save the leftovers (or cook a little extra) for kedgeree (page 98)
1 pound of smoked haddock
1-1/2 cups of milk (or cream)
Pepper
Butter (optional)
Baked potatoes, toast, or crackers

If your fish has the skin on it, peel it off. Check for bones and if you find any, pull them out. If it is necessary to remove more salt, shred the fish somewhat, lay the fish in cold water for a couple of hours before you cook it. Drain.

Put the fish and milk in a wide pan, and bring gradually to a simmer and cook until the fish is tender. Add pepper to taste, the optional butter, and serve in a soup plate over potatoes, toast, or crackers.

Serves 3-4.

BRANDADA DE BACALLA

Modern New Englanders are familiar with Mediterranean cookery in a degree that would astonish nineteenth-century people. Because of the copious garlic, this manner of preparing our traditional salt cod would have discomfited early Yankees who supplied the fish to the Spanish and French people who developed this dish in the first place. For us in the twenty-first century, it makes a good appetizer, and is a good way to use leftover salt cod from a boiled dinner. Make it a few hours before serving to allow the garlic flavor to develop and mellow.

3/4 cup of cooked salt cod
1 cup of boiled potatoes,
2 cloves of garlic
1/2 cup mild olive oil
Salt and pepper

Pick over the cod to make sure all the bones are out. Flake it. Mash the potatoes, and mince the garlic. Put the salt cod, potatoes, and garlic together in food processor, and puree them adding the oil gradually until the brandada absorbs it all.

Spread thickly on toast, crostini, or bagel chips.

Serves 8-12 as appetizer.

CLAM FRITTERS

CLAM FRITTERS (No. 2).

Strain one pint of clams, saving the juice; add to this juice sufficient water to make one pint; mix into it one egg, well beaten, and sufficient prepared flour to make a light batter, also the clams chopped, and some salt. Drop by the spoonful into boiling-hot lard.

From *Practical Cooking and Dinner Giving* by Mrs. Mary F. Henderson, 1882

BECAUSE THIS RECIPE CALLS for clam juice instead of milk, these fritters have a nice strong clam flavor. When you buy clams, keep in mind that if you order a pint you will get one generous cup of clams plus a cup of juice. This recipe has a high yield, and you may wish to halve it.

3-1/3 cups flour
2 teaspoons salt
5 teaspoons baking powder
Pepper to taste
1 egg
Clam juice with water added
  to make 2 cups
2 cups clams, strained and chopped

Put at least three inches of shortening in a heavy pan and heat till it is at 365° or a one-inch cube of bread will brown in 1 minute. Sift together dry ingredients. In a separate bowl, beat the egg well, and then mix in the clam juice and water. Stir the wet ingredients into the dry ingredients and beat with a spoon until you have a smooth batter, then mix in the clams and stir enough to distribute them evenly through the batter.

Drop the batter by large spoonfuls into the hot fat and cook for about three minutes each, or until they are golden brown all over. Cook only a few at a time so that they are not crowded in the pot. Remove and drain on paper towels. Keep finished fritters warm in the oven while you cook the rest.

Yields 30-40 fritters.

DEVILED LOBSTER OR CRAB

Deviled Lobster is made the same way as deviled crab, merely substituting the lobster for the crab, and adding a grating of nutmeg to the seasoning. In boiling lobsters and crabs, they are sufficiently cooked when they assume a bright red color. Too much boiling renders them tough.

From *Practical Cooking and Dinner Giving*, by Mrs. Henderson, 1882

BRINGING A WHOLE boiled lobster or crab to the dining table was just not done in the nineteenth century. That was how you ate lobster at the beach. At home, the meat was picked out and then seasoned, mixed with sauces and baked, or turned into a stew or salad. Deviling usually required some spicy addition, such as cayenne, or mustard.

One way to make an elegant presentation, enabling the diner to eat lobster without having to crack open messy shells at the table, was to pick the meat out of the lobster, keeping the shell as intact as possible. The tail section was made into a boat shape and the body cleaned out and laid open-side up. Deviled lobster meat was then spooned back inside, and the whole run under a broiler till golden. You may or may not wish to follow suit.

1 cup (6 ounces) cooked lobster or crabmeat
1/2 cup fresh bread crumbs
Two hard-boiled eggs, chopped (optional)
A grating or two of fresh nutmeg
1/4 teaspoon cayenne pepper (more to taste)
1 teaspoon dry mustard
Salt
Juice of half a lemon
2/3 cup hot cream sauce

Preheat the oven to 400°. Toss the shellfish meat together with the bread crumbs, chopped eggs, seasonings, and lemon juice. Stir hot cream sauce into the mixture until it is evenly moistened. Put into lobster shells, or ramekins and bake for 10 to 12 minutes or until it is bubbling. Put it under the broiler briefly to turn the top golden.

Serves 2-3 as main dish, or 4 as appetizer.

FRIED OYSTERS

Dry the oysters in a clean towel; then dip in beaten egg, and then in rolled crack-er crumbs; fry about five minutes in lard or beef drippings. Butter is apt to be too oily, and lard is better for frying them in.

From *Mrs. Winslow's Domestic Receipt Book for 1878*

NEXT TO STEWING AND scalloping, frying seems to have been the most popular method of preparing oysters in the nineteenth century. The earliest fried oyster recipes called for a batter that the oysters were dipped into before frying. But this simple egg and cracker batter is easy and delicious. I recommend using butter because it gives a wonderful flavor to the dish but for a real taste of the nineteenth-century, try lard or beef drippings.

If you cook this down hearth, use a fry pan set on a low trivet with plenty of fresh coals.

24 oysters
1 egg, beaten
1 cup crushed pilot crackers
Butter

Drain the raw shucked oysters and pat dry in a clean towel. Heat enough butter to cover the bottom of a heavy deep pan over a medium-low heat till it bubbles but does not turn brown.

Dip each oyster in the beaten egg, then in the cracker crumbs, and fry for about 1-1/2 minutes on each side. Drain on paper towels and keep warm in the oven before serving.

Yields 24 fried oysters.

HOWARD'S SILVER SPRING OYSTERS.

SCALLOPED OYSTERS

Ingredients: Three dozen oysters, a large tea-cupful of bread or cracker crumbs, two ounces of fresh butter, pepper and salt, half a tea-cupful of oyster juice. Make layers of these ingredients, as described in the last article, in the top of a chafing dish, or any kind of pudding or gratin dish; bake in a quick oven about fifteen minutes; brown with a salamander.

From *Practical Cooking and Dinner Giving,* by Mrs. Mary F. Henderson, 1882

THIS RECIPE PRODUCES a strong oyster taste. I found the recipe worked well with crushed oyster crackers, but any saltine or chowder cracker will do. Some period recipes recommend putting a few spoonfuls of milk or cream over each layer. This is good to do if you do not like a strong oyster flavor.

You can prepare this dish in a fireplace in a bake kettle.

1-1/2 cups of bread or cracker crumbs
1/4 cup melted butter
1 pint shucked oysters
1/4 cup oyster liquor
1/4 cup cream
Salt and pepper to taste

Preheat the oven to 425°. Grease a baking dish or casserole. Mix together the cracker crumbs and melted butter and sprinkle a third of them into the bottom of the dish. Put half of the oysters over that, drizzling half of the liquor plus the cream over them. Repeat. Top with the remaining one-third of the crumbs, and bake for about 30 minutes or until the oysters are firm, and the top is a golden brown. If necessary, run it under the broiler a few moments.

Serves four.

ROASTED OYSTERS

Select single oysters in the shell, and put them, with the rounded side down, upon a gridiron and over a sharp fire. They will roast in a very short time. Send them to the table in the shell, with coffee, cold-slaw, and fresh bread and butter.

From *The Practical Cookbook,* by Mrs. Bliss, 1864

THIS SET OF INSTRUCTIONS for the hearth cook makes a nice supper menu. You can also do this on your outdoor grill. My friend Ruth Stetson, who tried this method of cooking oysters, suggests "continuing dinner with a large stuffed fish, and corn-on-the-cob as long as your grill is hot," with French bread on the side. Cocktail sauce is good on the oysters.

Scrub the oysters well with a brush. Have a charcoal fire ready as hot as for steak. If you have a lidded grill, put the oysters on, close the lid, and roast them for only three minutes. Without a lid, you may wish to cook them a bit longer. If cooked too long, they will lose some of their liquid and be dry.

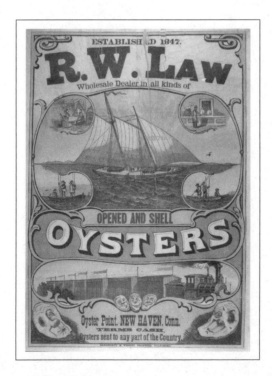

OYSTER FRICASSEE

Drain a quart of large oysters from their liquor, and place them in a covered saucepan with a quarter of a pound of good butter. Set them on the back of the range, and let them simmer gently until the oysters are well plumped out.

Put the oysters liquor in another saucepan with three tablespoonfuls of powdered cracker, and a little pepper. When the oysters are done, remove them from the butter with a fork, and place tem on toasted crackers on a hot platter. Add the butter in which they have been cooked to the oyster broth. Let it boil up once. Stir in half a pint of cream, and pour over the oysters.

From *The Century Cook Book* by Mary Ronald, 1906

---

1 stick of butter
1 quart shucked oysters drained,
   liquor reserved
3 tablespoons cracker crumbs
1 cup cream (or half-and-half)
Salt and pepper to taste
Additional crackers for serving
   or toasted bread.

Melt butter in a deep, heavy pan; when butter has melted, put in the oysters and cook until the edges curl. Put the oyster liquor in a separate pan with the cracker crumbs, and bring just to a boil.

Add the butter from the pan you cooked the oysters in, if you wish, and stir in the cream. Cook for three minutes until it is hot through. Add salt and pepper to taste.

Put crackers or toast in the bottom of a soup plate and serve the oysters over them.

Serves 4.

6 Vegetables

VEGETABLES ARE HELD IN HIGHER ESTEEM TODAY than perhaps they were in the nineteenth and early twentieth centuries. There are a number of reasons for this. One is that the hard work many people performed daily required plenty of carbohydrates and fat for fuel, so starchier vegetables like potatoes, turnips, squash, and corn were preferred over vegetables like green beans, asparagus, and lettuce. Also, vegetable growing is labor intensive, so plants that fared well with little attention, like radishes and beets, were preferred over ones requiring staking and pruning like tomatoes. The seasonal nature of vegetable growing in a cool climate meant people showed a preference for cool weather tolerant vegetables like cabbage, and those that stored well, like roots and winter squashes over the fleeting pleasures of shorter-season vegetables.

Still we know that each fresh vegetable was greeted with pleasure as it appeared in season, and diary keepers note with apparent pride and enjoyment the first green peas, the new beans, and fresh corn. People shared abundant fresh vegetables or even gathered with friends and family to enjoy them. Others were pickled for use later. The following recipes advise you on preparing some of New England's favorites.

BAKED BEANS

Examine and wash one quart of dry beans (the pea bean is the best), and put them in a pan with six quarts of cold water; let them soak in this over night. In the morning wash them in another water, and place them on the fire with six quarts of cold water and a pound of mixed salt pork. If they are the present year's beans, they will cook enough in half and hour; if older, one hour. Drain them and put half in the bean-pot; then gash the pork and put in the remainder of the beans, one tablespoon of molasses, and one of salt, and cover with boiling water. Bake ten hours. Watch them carefully, and do not let them cook dry.

From *The Appledore Cook Book,* by Maria Parloa, 1880

FEW NINETEENTH-CENTURY cookbooks show recipes for baked beans, but since there is considerable evidence that people ate them, they seem to have been one of the dishes cooks assembled by eye. When instructions *are* given, the ratio of one quart of beans to one pound of salt pork is common. Molasses seldom appears until the last quarter of the century, and then only a tablespoonful per quart of beans, a good deal less than we use now.

The salt pork used would have been leaner than today. Mrs. Child said "Pieces of pork alternately fat and lean are the most suitable; the cheeks are the best." Of course, you will be hard pressed to find cheeks in the meat case of the modern grocery store. When served, the dish was presented with the meat on a platter of its own or in a dish with the beans all around.

Modern people will be startled at non-sweet early-style pork and beans. We are so accustomed to molasses and/or brown sugar, onion, and mustard that you may wish to add brown sugar or more molasses. Prepared the old way, it is a simple and economical dish.

If you have a fireplace bake oven, you may wish to bake your beans in that after you have finished with bread and pies. Recheck the oven from time to time to make sure the temperature has not dropped much below 225°, and if it has, put a couple of shovels full of coals in the oven. If you do not wish to use the oven, set the bean pot at the side of the hearth, where it will stay hot, turning it about every half hour to make sure one side does not scorch. You can also slow-cook the beans in a bake kettle or Dutch oven on coals, or hung high over the fire.

2 lbs. Navy beans
5 quarts of water, twice
1/2 pound of lean salt pork, cut through
**   to the rind in several places**
1/4 cup molasses
1 tablespoon salt
Pepper (optional)
Onion (optional)

In a large kettle, soak the beans overnight. In the morning, drain them, put in another five quarts of fresh water and bring them to a boil, checking after 30 minutes to see if the skins will break when you blow on them. When they do, spoon the beans into a bean pot, burying the salt pork in the middle, add the molasses, salt, pepper, and onion. Add enough cooking water so that the beans are barely covered, and put into a 225° oven for six to eight hours, or longer in a 200° oven. Check to make sure they do not dry out, and for the last hour, pull the pork to the top to brown.

Yields about a gallon of beans.

CELERY

Scrape and wash it well; let it lie in cold water until just before being used; dry it with a cloth; trim it, and split down the stalks almost to the bottom. Send to table in a celery glass, and eat it with salt only; or chop it fine, and make a salad dressing for it.

From *Practical American Cookery and Domestic Economy,* by Miss Hall, 1855

CELERY WAS A SPECIAL-occasion food for much of the 1800s with enough status to warrant its own specific serving glass in which it graced Thanksgiving, Christmas, and other festive tables. Celery, according to Mrs. Child in 1833, was harvested whole, and stored with the roots kept damp, but it probably lost some moisture, requiring the soaking specified by Miss Hall.

COLD SLAW

Shred a white cabbage and pour over it the following.

Dressing

2 beaten eggs; 2 teaspoonfuls of sugar; 6 tablespoonfuls of vinegar; 1/2 teaspoon of made mustard and same of pepper and salt; 1/2 teaspoonful of celery essence; 1 tablespoonful of butter.

Mix well, stir over the fire until scalding hot. When cold add the cabbage. Toss and stir, and set in a cold place until wanted.

From *Practical Cooking and Dinner Giving*, by Marion Harland, 1882

MANY OLD SLAW RECIPES are called "cold" slaw, a misinterpretation of the spoken word cole. This recipe is more a set of instructions for a salad dressing than for a slaw and it produces a peppery, somewhat tangy sweet-and-sour dressing. Made-mustard merely means a prepared mustard of the sort we regularly purchase. I like to use a Dijon style.

2 eggs beaten
2 teaspoons of sugar
6 tablespoons of cider vinegar
1/2 teaspoon of mustard
1/2 teaspoon ground celery seed
1 tablespoon butter or olive oil.
Salt and pepper to taste
1 small head of cabbage, shredded.

Combine everything except the cabbage in a double boiler and cook over a low heat for five minutes whisking frequently. Once it begins to thicken, it finishes very quickly. Let it cool somewhat and then pour it over the shredded cabbage until there is enough to your taste. Put in fridge to chill before serving.

Yields 3/4-cup dressing.

HULLED CORN

Put two handfuls of clean hard-wood ashes in two quarts of cold water; boil fifteen or twenty minutes; let stand until the ashes settle and the water is perfectly clear. To this cleansed water (it should be strong enough of the lye to feel a little slippery), add as much cold water as is necessary to cover the corn. Put the corn in the water; let it boil until the hulls begin to start, then skim the corn out into a pan of clear, cold water, and rub thoroughly with the hands to remove the hulls and cleanse the corn from the lye,—rub it through two or three, or even four waters, that there may be no taste of lye; then put into clear water and boil until tender.

From *Mrs. Rorer's Philadelphia Cook Book,* by Mrs. S.T. Rorer, 1886

MRS. RORER EXPLAINED that hulled corn is "corn soaked in an alkali to remove the hull." "Hulling" was a good way to make a breakfast food or vegetable side dish out of long-keeping dried corn. Corn and its various preparations have more regional names than nearly any other food item. Today hulled corn is generally called hominy and can be purchased canned. In nineteenth-century New England it was made and peddled by the "samp man," but it was also termed simply "hulled corn." Sea captain's wife Mary Lawrence recorded that she made hulled corn on board the whaleship *Addison.*

One half gallon of water
1/4 cup of baking soda
1 quart of dried corn

Put the water in a deep, non-reactive kettle with the baking soda and stir until the soda is dissolved. Add the corn and allow it to soak overnight. The next day, bring the soaking corn just to a boil, and then take it off the heat and drain. Put the corn into clean cold water and rub the corn kernels briskly between your hands to loosen the hulls which will float to the surface. Periodically change the water, and continue rubbing until most kernels seem to lack hulls. If necessary, mix fresh soaking liquid and allow the corn to soak again for a few hours.

Rinse the corn thoroughly in fresh water, and boil it in fresh water until the kernels are puffed and tender. Serve as a side dish with butter, salt and pepper, or use as an ingredient in succotash.

CORN OYSTERS

Grate young sweet corn, and to a pint add one egg well beaten, small teacup of flour, half gill of cream or milk, and a teaspoonful of salt; mix well together, drop into the fat by spoonfuls about the size of an oyster. If you are all run down Hood's Sarsaparilla will build you up.

From *Hood's Combined Cook Books,* by C.I. Hood & Co., 1875-1885, High Street

THESE DO INDEED LOOK like fried oysters. In the fritter tradition, they are a delicious vegetable accompaniment to any summer meal. Every year I dedicate one batch of freshly picked corn to the corn oysters that we eagerly anticipate. They are best made from fresh, uncooked corn, if you can bear having corn some other way besides on the cob.

2 cups grated fresh sweet corn
1 egg beaten
1/2 cup flour
1/4 cup cream or milk
1 teaspoon salt

Mix together corn, egg, and milk and add the flour gradually. Drop by table-spoons-full onto a very well oiled griddle and fry quickly, turning them once. Drain on paper and keep warm in the oven until served.

Yields about a dozen and serves four as a side dish.

Sometimes called Quaker Corn. It cannot be excelled in tenderness, or sweetness. Kernels closely packed on the cob. Bears several ears to each stalk. Small cob. ¼ bu.75, ⅛ bu.40, qt.35, pt.20, ½ pt.12.

SUCCOTASH

Take one pint of shelled green lima beans, wash, cover with hot water, let stand for five minutes, pour off water, and place beans in hot water over fire; boil fifteen minutes. Prepare six good sized ears of corn, by cutting down carefully, add to beans; boil half an hour, add pepper, salt, and two tablespoonfuls of butter. Watch that it does not scorch. Or, to cook with meat, boil one pint of salt pork two hours, add beans, cook fifteen minutes, then add corn, omitting butter.

From *Food for the Hungry: A Complete Manual...,*compiled by Julia Wright, 1896

SUCCOTASH

Cut hot boiled corn from cob, add equal quantity of hot boiled shelled beans; season with butter and salt; reheat before serving.

From *The Boston Cooking School Cookbook*, by Fannie Merritt Farmer, 1896

THESE TWO SUCCOTASH recipes, only two of many published in the late 1800s, show how many variations could be played on the theme of beans and corn. These recipes all assume the use of fresh corn off the cob or canned sweet corn. Most succotash recipes call for stewing the corn with shelled horticultural or lima beans. Strictly speaking this version of succotash would be a summer-only dish, unless canned corn and beans were used.

There is no mystery to succotash. Equal quantities of corn and beans is the usual, but if you prefer one over the other, use more of your favorite. For a meaty dish, you certainly can use lean salt pork as you might for baked beans. Some recipes recommend cooking the kernelless cobs in the pan with the corn and beans which intensifies the flavor. Remember to take them out before serving. I personally like the modern touch of onion in my succotash.

3 ears fresh corn on the cob or one cup of hulled corn (page 111)
1 cup fresh shell beans (or canned or frozen shell beans or limas)
Water
1 tablespoon butter
Salt and pepper
Small piece of salt pork (optional)

Cut the corn from the cobs, scraping the cob with the back of your knife to get all the little bits of kernel. Put corn and beans into a heavy saucepan and add only enough water that you can barely see through the mixture. If you use salt pork, add it now. Simmer the mixture for half an hour, or, if you used fresh beans, until the shell beans are tender. Add butter, salt and pepper to taste. Some people add a splash of milk or cream. Succotash is often better the second day.

Succotash is delicious cooked on a hearth fire. You can use the same earthenware pot that you use for baked beans, set at the side of the fire, or cook it in an iron pot hung high enough to prevent scorching.

Yields four servings.

LETTUCE SALAD

LETTUCE. Strip off the outside leaves, split it and lay in cold water awhile. Drain and lay in a salad dish. Have ready two hardboiled eggs, cut in two, and lay on the leaves. If you choose, it may be dressed with sugar and vinegar, with a little salt, before it goes to the table. Some prefer a dressing of salt, mustard, loaf sugar, and vinegar, sweet oil, and a mashed hard boiled egg. With the salad cut fine, and this over it.

From *The Complete Domestic Guide*, by Mrs. L.G. Abell, 1853

THE PHRASE "LETTUCE SALAD" might sound redundant to modern people. We are so accustomed today to lettuce or mixed greens presented in a large bowl or on individual plates, with perhaps a slice or two of tomato, a bit of cucumber that when we say salad, that is what comes to mind. In the nineteenth century, the word salad often referred to cold food, often meat or seafood, served with a dressing, sometimes on lettuce. Hard boiled eggs often garnished the plate or were incorporated into the salad.

This set of instructions actually contains several ways of preparing a lettuce salad, each worth trying for their own sakes, but also as interesting examples of nineteenth-century food habits.

Most of us today use a prepared salad dressing of one style or another, but nineteenth-century tables often sported cruet sets with bottles for oil, vinegar, or catsup and shakers for salt, pepper, dry mustard, and sugar. A diner could dress his or her own salad at the table from the castor's containers. Also the cook could sprinkle the oil and vinegar, shake some salt, pepper and sugar over it. "Sweet oil" was the name for olive oil at this time, and "Loaf sugar" was white sugar.

The cook could also make a vinaigrette of oil, vinegar, and mustard, into which mashed hard boiled egg was mixed, and added to the salad before it was served.

ONIONS

PICK SMALL ONIONS for this recipe. At the holidays it is very common to find small boiling onions for creamed onions. Remove the skins easily by blanching them in hot water until the skins slip off easily when you take off the top and bottom and pinch the onion. To finish cooking them, simply simmer in equal quantities of milk and water, and drain them or use the cooking liquid as a base for a cream sauce.

The milk in this dish is susceptible to taking on the odor of smoke when it is prepared in the fireplace. You may enjoy that, but if you are doubtful whether you will, after boiling the onions put them in a pan with a tight-fitting lid at the side of the fire over a small bed of coals until you serve them.

SWEET POTATOES

Sweet potatoes should never be pared before cooking. If you wish to boil them, wash them clean, cut a bit from each end, and boil in clear water, without salt; the water in the boiling pot should always boil before the potatoes are put in; large potatoes require one hour to boil.

From *The Practical Cookbook*, by Mrs. Bliss, 1864

Wash them perfectly clean, wipe them dry, and bake in a quick oven, according to their size—half an hour for quite small size, three-quarters for larger, and a full hour for the largest. Let the oven have a good heat, and do not open it, unless it is necessary to turn them, until they are done.

From *Practical American Cookery and Domestic Economy*, by Elizabeth M. Hall, 1855

ALTHOUGH MORE DIFFICULT to grow in New England than in the South, sweet potatoes were familiar to the Yankees who bought them in foreign ports and ate them aboard sailing vessels all around the world. In the North, white, or Irish potatoes were most common, but sweet potatoes had been used in English cookery in the eighteenth century, often in puddings. Aboard ship either boiling or baking sweet potatoes was possible, and I give the edge to boiling. Personally, I like them baked and would follow Miss Hall's advice any day.

If you cook these in a fireplace, you can put them either into the oven around the edges while other items are baking, or on a rack in a bake kettle for the same amount of time as in a conventional oven.

BAKED SWEET POTATOES

1 medium sweet potato per person

Preheat the oven to 350°. Scrub the potatoes and lightly oil the skins. Set on a rack in the center of the oven for 45 minutes, test with a knife for doneness.

POTATOES

Potatoes were served with virtually every meal in nineteenth-century New England, usually boiled, sometimes mashed, and leftovers were fried up for supper or breakfast. Recipes books of the era offered up all sorts of ways to scallop or cream them, even make soufflés.

Fireplace cooks will find boiling potatoes over fire as easy as on a stove, but there are a couple other ways to use the fire to cook potatoes. One is to bury the potato deep in ashes at the side of the fire. You can cover the spot with fresh coals, but be careful not to scorch the potato. To eat it, dust the exterior, and cut it in half and scoop out the cooked potato.

In *Common Sense in the Household* Marion Harland suggested, "cut whole boiled potatoes lengthwise, into slices a quarter of an inch thick, and lay on a gridiron over a hot, bright, fire. Brown on both sides, sprinkle with pepper and salt, lay a bit of butter upon each, and eat very hot."

When you roast a piece of meat before the fire, have potatoes cut up in chunks, and put them in the bottom of the tin kitchen or in a dripping pan. Let them cook and the roasting meat will baste them. Stir them from time to time. You can do the same thing in a conventional oven.

TURNIPS

For Turnip Sauce. — Boil your turnips and mash them fine; add the same amount of mealy mashed potatoes; season with salt and pepper, moisten it with cream or butter.

From *New England Economical Housekeeper*, by Mrs. E.A. Howland

THE COMBINATION OF potatoes and turnips cuts the strong flavor of turnip that some people object to. In Scotland this combination is called clapshot, and the yellow (Swede) turnip, rutabaga, is used. Either purple-topped white turnips or rutabagas are good fixed this way. The term "sauce" was used in earlier days to refer to cooked vegetables and does not mean that this should be sauce-like in texture.

This is a flexible recipe, because while the recipe says equal parts of potato and turnip, in fact, you can use more of one than the other and still make a delicious dish. The cream is not necessary.

2 cups of boiled, potatoes
2 cups of boiled turnips or rutabaga
1/4 cup cream or 4 tablespoons
of butter
Salt and pepper

Mix the two vegetables together in a large pan, with a bit of liquid and heat them until they are hot. Drain and mash them together, and add the cream or butter, salt and pepper to taste. Serve immediately.

Serves 4-6.

The old well known standard variety for table use, and general crop for feeding to stock. Splendid keepers; productive; fine for market. Sow 2 to 3 ℔s per acre. ℔.40, ½℔.25, ¼℔.15, oz.6, pkt.4.

STEWING TOMATOES

In stewing tomatoes, pour away the surplus water, so soon as they begin to boil, and add a small piece of butter, a very little sugar, pepper, and salt; cook about 15 minutes, then stir in bread crumbs, if you like them. Hood's Vegetable Pills cure constipation.

From *Hood's Combined Cook Books*, by C.I. Hood & Co., 1875-1885, Hood's #3

TOMATOES TAKE CANNING well, both domestically and industrially. Mrs. Harland in *The Dinner Year Book* wrote in her stewed-tomato recipe: "Open a can of tomatoes an hour before cooking them." She also recommended that the cook "Leave out the cores and unripe parts. Cook them always in tin or porcelain saucepans. Iron injures color and flavor."

Modern people like raw tomatoes so much, and make every effort to have them fresh year round. Cooked tomatoes now seem relegated to pasta sauces and casseroles. Nineteenth-century New Englanders certainly did eat raw tomatoes in season, but preferred them cooked.

Dry bread crumbs work best because they do not get as mushy as fresh ones do; merely sprinkle them into the pan. If you use canned tomatoes, read the label to see if sugar has already been added. If you use fresh tomatoes, taste before you add the sugar. Modern tomato breeding has created sweeter tomatoes than were available 100 years ago.

2 cups of stewed tomatoes, drained
1 tablespoon of butter
Salt and pepper to taste
Sugar (optional)
2 tablespoons dry bread crumbs

Empty the drained tomatoes into a non-reactive pan, and put over a low heat for about ten minutes. Add the butter, salt and pepper; taste for sweetness and add sugar if needed. Just before serving, sprinkle in the bread crumbs.

Serves 4.

7 Desserts

THE NINETEENTH CENTURY TRULY INDULGED the American sweet tooth, and New Englanders heartily joined in. Cheaper sugar, conveniences such as semi-instant gelatin, ice boxes, and cranked ice cream machines put fancy molded and chilled desserts into the hands of middle-class people for special occasions, while ordinary family cooks made charming but more homely steamed puddings with sweet sauces and comforting desserts like apple dumplings and bread pudding.

Fireplace cooks will find nearly all the steamed or baked puddings or the shortcakes good for the end of a hearth cooked meal.

AMBROSIAS

Orange Ambrosia

8 fine oranges, peeled and sliced.
1/2 grated coconut.
1/2 cup of powdered sugar.

Arrange slices of orange in a glass dish; scatter grated coconut thickly over them; sprinkle this lightly with sugar, and cover with another layer of orange. Fill the dish in this order, having a double quantity of coconut at top. Serve soon after it is prepared.

From *The Dinner Year Book*, by Marion Harland, 1878

Pine-apple Ambrosia

1 pine-apple, pared and cut into small squares.
1 coconut, pared and grated.
1 cup powdered sugar.
1 large glass good sherry or Marsala.

Put a layer of pineapple in a glass bowl; strew with sugar, and wet with wine. Next, put a stratum of coconut, and sprinkle more sparsely with sugar. More pineapple, sugar, and wine, and continue to add layers in the order given. The top coating must be of coconut. Eat soon, or the pineapple will wither in the wine and become tough. Pass light cake with it.

From *The Dinner Year Book*, by Marion Harland, 1878

SEAFARERS OFTEN REMARKED on the succulence of fresh tropical fruits. In the last half of the nineteenth century these exotics were increasingly available in fresh condition in New England towns. Still, oranges were a special treat for many people, and so were pineapples.

These two ambrosia recipes are wonderfully simple and depend upon fresh coconut and fruit for success. As it stands, the pineapple ambrosia has a strong coconut flavor. One average-sized coconut will yield about six cups of fresh grated coconut while one pineapple yields about four cups. You may wish to reduce the coconut by half or more.

Use confectioners sugar or granulated sugar powdered in a blender and adjust the amount to your taste, keeping in mind that nineteenth-century Yankees had a sweet tooth. A large glass of sherry is about half a cup; a medium golden sherry is a good choice.

The orange ambrosia serves 8-10.
The pineapple ambrosia serves 4.

INDIAN PUDDING

Scald the milk, and stir in the sifted meal to make a batter not very thick. Then add two spoonsful of flour, molasses to your taste, a little salt, lemon, nutmeg, or cinnamon, and bake two hours and a half. Made in this way, it is quite as good as when made with eggs

From *The Complete Domestic Guide,* by Mrs. L.G. Abell, 1853

INDIAN PUDDING IS a much-neglected dessert nowadays, even in New England where it was a traditional dish. One secret to a really good Indian pudding is using stone ground corn meal, avoiding corn meals with a granular texture. Indian pudding recipes varied a great deal in the past, some calling for eggs, some for flour, with lesser or greater amounts of milk or sweetening. When this pudding is baked you will notice that there is a thicker portion and a more liquid portion. This is a desirable mixture and a combination must be spooned into serving dishes.

Indian pudding is easily baked in a bee-hive oven along with the baked beans since both require a low temperature.

4 cups of milk plus 2 cups
1/2 cup cornmeal
1 teaspoon salt
2 tablespoons flour
1 tablespoon cinnamon or ginger,
**   or a combination of the two**
1/2 cup molasses
1/4 cup white sugar (optional)

Preheat oven to 300°. Grease a two-quart baking dish. Scald a quart of milk in a double boiler. Whisk the cornmeal salt, flour, and spice mixed into one cup cold milk to make a thin batter. Pour it into the scalded milk, and cook this mixture for 20 minutes, stirring it frequently especially in the last ten minutes of cooking. Take it off the heat and add the molasses whisking it gradually into the scalded milk and cornmeal. Taste, and add the white sugar if you wish additional sweetness. Make sure it is uniformly mixed.

Pour into the baking dish. Spoon the remaining one cup of cold milk over the top without mixing it in. Bake for 2-1/2 to 3 hours. Serve warm with cream or vanilla ice cream.

Serves 8.

QUEEN OF PUDDING

One pint of nice bread crumbs, one quart of milk, one cup of sugar, the yolks of four eggs, the grated rind of one lemon, a piece of butter the size of an egg. Bake like a custard. When baked spread over the top slices of jelly of any kind, and cover the whole with the whites of the eggs beaten to a stiff froth, with one cup of sugar and the juice of the lemon. Brown slightly in the oven.

From *Hood's Combined Cookbooks* by C.I. Hood and Co., 1885-1895, *Hood's #1*

IT IS A SHAME THAT this elegant, delicious, and popular nineteenth-century pudding should have virtually disappeared, although occasionally modern variations appear. Revived during Victoria's reign, and named for her, it is a variation on an earlier bread pudding. People who do not usually enjoy bread pudding like the custard-like quality of this recipe. The colorful jelly layer and meringue top make it very dressy.

One period recipe for queen of pudding suggests using currant jelly; a tart jelly is certainly better than sweet jelly or jam. If you have no stale bread for the crumbs use firm white bread grated in a food processor or blender and dried briefly in the oven.

You can bake this in a beehive oven, but using a conventional oven is easier.

PUDDING

1 quart of milk
2 cups of stale white bread crumbs
1 cup sugar
2 tablespoons of butter
4 eggs separated
Grated rind of one lemon
Topping
1 cup tart jelly, your choice of flavor
Reserved whites of four eggs
1/2 cup of sugar
Pinch of cream of tartar

Preheat oven to 350°. Grease a glass or oven-proof pudding dish, and heat some water to make a hot water bath for the pudding. In a separate bowl, set the crumbs to soak in the milk. In another bowl, cream together the sugar and butter, and beat in the egg yolks and the lemon rind. Turn the soaked crumbs into the egg and sugar mixture, and blend well. Pour it into the baking dish, and set the baking dish in a pan of hot water. Place it in the center of the oven. Bake for one hour and ten minutes or until it is set in the middle.

Take it out of the oven and allow to cool. Put as much jelly as you like over the top of the pudding. You will not be able to spread it, so the old recipe's instructions for "slices" is appropriate. If you cannot remove the jelly from its jar in one mass, then you will have to scoop off thin slices with a spoon to lay on the pudding.

Beat the whites of the four eggs, gradually adding the sugar and lemon juice. Spread this over the jelly-topped pudding and run it back into a 350° oven for 10-12 minutes or until slightly browned on top.

Serve cold.

Serves 8-10.

GINGERBREAD PUDDING

Three and a half cups flour, half a cup butter, one and a half cup milk, one cup molasses, one teaspoon soda. Steam three hours. Sauce.

If condensed milk is used do not put in quite as much molasses.

From the Logbook of the schooner *William B. Herrick*, 1874-76, Log 713, G.W. Blunt White Library

THIS STEAMED PUDDING has the consistency of a dense, moist cake and could have easily been made in the *Herrick*'s galley. The recipe is another example of a manuscript source that omits the obvious seasoning—in this case, ginger—something rarely done by writers of published cookbooks. The note about condensed milk improves the probability that the *Herrick* recipes were actually used at sea. Canned condensed milk was a very common item in the provisioning lists of sailing vessels in the last part of the nineteenth century and would have been the obvious substitute for fresh milk.

3-1/2 cups of flour
1 teaspoon baking soda
2 teaspoons ginger
1/2 cup butter
1/2 cup milk
1 cup molasses

Set a pot of water on the stove to boil. Grease a pudding mold or pudding bowl. Mix together the flour, baking soda, and ginger. Cut in the butter. Mix in the molasses and milk. Pour the batter into the pudding mold, and fasten the top or tie a dampened cloth over the top of the mold or bowl.

Set the mold in the boiling water, so that the water comes about halfway up the side of the bowl. Steam for 2 hours, then test as you would for a cake, and steam longer if the tester does not come out clean.

Turn it out while it is warm, and allow to cool. Serve with whipped or sweetened cream.

Yields one large pudding.

SNOW PUDDING

Whipped Jelly or Snow Pudding

Make a wine or lemon jelly … Place it in a bowl on ice; when it is cold but before it begins to harden, beat it with a Dover beater until it becomes white and a mass of froth. Turn it into a mold to harden. Serve it with a sauce made of boiled custard or any preserve that will go well with the flavoring or a compote of orange or any fruit.

From *The Century Cook Book* by Mary Ronald, 1906

IN PRE-EGG BEATER days fancy desserts like snow puddings took time and effort so once egg beaters were invented and sold widely, showy desserts like snows became common even in middle-class homes. Modern cooks can use electric beaters, so making this pudding today is a great deal easier than for nineteenth-century cooks. This recipe makes a lovely-looking pudding, especially if you chill it in a mold. It has a light texture and refreshing flavor, a nice light dessert after a heavy meal.

Garnish with berries, whipped cream, dots of jelly, candied fruit, or the ambrosia on page 122.

SNOW

1 tablespoon gelatin
1/4 cup cold water
1 cup boiling water
1 cup sugar
Juice of one and a half lemons
3 egg whites

Soak gelatin in cold water. When dissolved, add the boiling water, sugar, and lemon juice. Chill till it is mostly set up. Beat the whites of the eggs until very frothy then gradually add the chilled gelatin mixture. Beat constantly till all the gelatin mixture is added and is fluffy. Pour into a two-quart mold and chill until it is solid.

Custard:

1 cup milk
1/4 cup sugar
3 egg yolks
Zest of one lemon or
**   1 teaspoon vanilla extract**

Scald the milk in a double boiler over boiling water. Add sugar and stir to dissolve. Beat the yolks in a separate bowl, and spoon some of the hot milk into it and when it is well-blended, whisk it back into the rest of the milk, and cook over the boiling water until it coats the back of a spoon (about ten minutes). Stir in lemon zest or vanilla. Chill before serving.

To serve, unmold the snow by holding the mold in hot water a moment, or wrapping in a hot towel, turn it out on a platter, and pour the custard over and/or around the pudding. Garnish.

Serves six.

STEAMED PUDDING WITH LEMON DIP

Steam Pudding — Three cups flour; one cup of suet; one cup of raisins; one cup of molasses; two cups of milk; one teaspoonful of bicarbonate of soda. Chop the suet very fine, put it in the flour with the other ingredients, and steam it two hours. To be eaten with lemon dip.

Lemon Dip — Thin two tablespoonsful of flour with water; stir it into a pint of boiling water; let it boil once; take it up and stir in four tablespoonsful of sugar, a little butter, and the juice of one lemon. Some prefer wine or brandy dip, but teetotalers prefer the aforesaid lemon dip.

From the Mystic *Pioneer,* April 1859

TEMPERANCE AND diet reformers often recognized the importance of offering alternatives to prevalent usage and, as a result, countless lemons gave up their juice to battle rum or—in the case of pudding sauce—wine. This recipe is a standard suet-pudding recipe, suitable for everyday use, and just as likely to be served, despite the editor's special comment to teetotalers, with either a lemon or wine sauce. It would have been steamed in a pudding pan, bowl, or mold. The lemon dip is a flour-thickened sauce.

PUDDING

3 cups flour
1 teaspoon baking soda
1 cup grated suet
1 cup molasses
2 cups of milk
1 cup of raisins

Set a pot of water on the stove to boil. Grease a pudding mold or pudding bowl. Mix together the flour and baking soda and cut in the grated suet. Mix in the molasses and milk, and fold in the raisins. Pour the batter into the pudding mold, and fasten the top or tie a dampened cloth over the top of the mold or bowl.

Set the mold in the boiling water, so that the water comes about halfway up the side of the bowl. Steam for 1-1/2 hours, then test as you would for a cake, and steam longer if the tester does not come out clean.

When done, turn it out while it is still warm. Best served warm with lemon sauce. Use lemon sauce recipe on page 128.

Serves 6-8.

COTTAGE PUDDING

One cup sugar, one cup milk, two eggs, one pint flour, two teaspoon cream of tartar, one teaspoon soda, butter the size of an egg, little salt. Make and serve with wine Sauce.

Sauce half a cup of sugar piece of butter size of an egg and little wine or nutmeg and extract lemon.

From the logbook of the schooner *William B. Herrick,* 1874-76, Log 713, G.W. Blunt White Library

HERE IS ANOTHER of the *Herrick* recipes. Easy and quick to make, it could be frosted or served with a sauce as suggested. In fact, without a sauce it has little character. Lemon extract frequently appears in provision lists —24 bottles of it on the legendary fishing schooner *Columbia*. When I tested this recipe, I made lemon sauce, which I personally prefer over wine sauce, and found this to be a pleasant dessert. It rises nicely, but has a coarse texture.

COTTAGE PUDDING

2 cups flour
2 teaspoons cream of tartar
1 teaspoon baking soda
1 cup sugar
1 cup milk
2 eggs
2 tablespoons melted butter

Preheat oven to 400°. Grease an 8" x 8" pan. Sift together the dry ingredients including the sugar. Mix together milk, eggs, and butter. Stir wet ingredients into the dry ingredients and stir to blend. Pour into the pan, and bake for 30 minutes, or until a tester inserted comes out clean.

LEMON SAUCE

1/2 cup sugar
2 tablespoons butter
Nutmeg to taste
1/2 teaspoon lemon extract
**   (or grated rind of one lemon)**

While the pudding is baking, melt the butter and add the sugar to it, cooking over a low flame until the mixture is translucent. Remove from heat and add the nutmeg and lemon extract or rind. Mix. Serve over the warm pudding.

Serves 6-8.

CHRISTMAS PUDDING

To bread crumbs and flour, three ounces of each,
Add three eggs and six ounces of suet
Chopped fine, and one-sixth of a nutmeg or more,
So long as you don't overdo it.
A good pinch of mace, and of cinnamon ground,
Or in other words carefully grated;
Half a pint of new milk, a spoonful of salt —
A teaspoon I ought to have stated.
To this add some raisins (Malaga) well stoned,
And some currants washed clean and washed nicely,
Of each half a pound, or as some people say,
Of either eight ounces precisely.
Then of citron and lemon an ounce and a half,
Half the former, and one of the latter;
Four ounces of sugar — the moist kind will do —
Which will form an exceeding rich batter
Or mixture. The eggs to a cream should be beat
With the spices, and then by degrees
The milk may be added according to taste,
And the other ingredient to please.
Now taking for granted the pudding is made,
And the water is boiling like fun;
Tie it up in a cloth, pop it into the pot,
And boil — seven hours — till done.

From *"Receipts, &c.," Godey's Lady's Book*, December 1857

THIS RHYMING RECIPE from *Godey*'s is one of several for various holiday treats. Holiday puddings can be boiled in pudding basins or molds, ceramic or metal, or in cloth bags. Molds are more decorative and make it easier to manage the steaming process. Boiling in bags à la Mrs. Cratchit in the *Christmas Carol* by Charles Dickens makes a homely pudding and requires practice.

This recipe really does make "an exceeding rich batter"—a very dark, very rich pudding which is not beautiful sitting all alone on a plate. Dredge it with some confectioners sugar and stick some holly in it to spruce it up. The flavor is very good.

If you decide to boil it in a bag, saturate the cloth with hot water, and dredge it thoroughly with flour. Maintain a constant level of water in the pot, adding water from a hot teakettle, and don't allow the bag to hit the bottom of the pot. You can keep the bag suspended by tying it with a string from a long handled-wooden spoon or a stick resting across the top of the pot.

3 eggs
1 teaspoon nutmeg
1/8 teaspoon mace
1/2 teaspoon cinnamon
1 cup milk
1/2 cup flour
1-1/3 cup bread crumbs
1-1/2 cups suet, grated
1 teaspoon salt
1-1/2 cups raisins
1-1/2 cups currants
2 tablespoons citron
Peel of 4 lemons, grated
1/2 cup brown sugar

Set a large kettle of water to boil. In a large bowl, beat the eggs with the spices and gradually add the milk. Add everything else, and mix together till well blended. Grease your pudding bowl, mold, or cloth (see directions on page 125). Empty the pudding into it, allowing room for the pudding to swell.

Boil or steam for five hours. If you boil the pudding in a bag, don't worry about a scum which may form as the suet melts a bit and soaks out through the bag.

Turn out on a platter, and serve warm, with a dusting of confectioners sugar, or flame it for presentation. (To flame the pudding, heat a quarter of a cup of brandy in a saucepan until it is just warm. Scoop out a spoonful and hold a lighted match near it. When a blue flame appears in the spoon, drizzle the rest of the warm brandy over the pudding and pour a spoon full on the pudding to catch all the brandy on fire.)

Serves 24.

PLUM BREAD PUDDING

Quaking Plum Pudding, very nice. Take slices of light bread and spread them thin with butter, and lay in the pudding dish layers of bread and raisins, within an inch of the top; then take five eggs and beat them well, and mix them with a quart of milk, and pour it over the pudding; add salt and spice to suit your taste; you may put in a cup of sugar and eat it with butter, or you may omit the sugar, and serve it up with sweet sauce. Bake it twenty or twenty-five minutes. Before you use the raisins, boil them in a very little water, and put it all in.

From *New England Economical Housekeeper,* by Mrs. E.A. Howland, 1845

RAISINS WERE THE "plums" in early recipes. Plum puddings, plum duff, plum cakes all call for raisins which in the pre-seedless-raisin era, were larger than modern raisins, and approached the size of small dried plums. Mrs. Howland's suggestions about serving this pudding with butter versus a sweet sauce reminds us that nineteenth-century puddings were seldom served without sauce. Although I recommend one cup of raisins in the interpretation that follows, there is no reason why you could not put in more if you like them.

If you bake this pudding only 25 minutes the custard will not be set, and it will truly quake. If you think you would prefer a firm pudding, bake it according to the time suggested.

6 slices of firm white bread
Butter
1 cup raisins soaked in
  1/2 cup hot water
5 eggs
1 quart milk
1/2 cup sugar, brown or white
1 teaspoon cinnamon
1/4 freshly grated nutmeg
Salt to taste

Preheat oven to 325°. Butter both sides of the bread and place the slices in a greased two-quart baking dish with raisins sprinkled generously between the layers of bread. Beat the eggs and add the milk, sugar, salt, and spices and beat all together. Pour the mixture over the bread. Allow it rest for 30 minutes before baking it.

Bake for 45-50 minutes or until it puffs. Serve warm or cold.

Serves 6-8.

BREAD PUDDING

Take a brick loaf
spread six slices with butter
lay these one by one in your dish
a cup of currants sprinkled
between each slice 3 eggs
to a pint & half of milk

Harriot Goddard Diary, Coll. 238 G.W. Blunt White Library, Mystic Seaport

THIS IS A VARIATION on the recipe above, using currants instead of raisins. It is from a manuscript source and typically is scant on details such as sweetening or seasoning. It is unlikely that Mrs. Goddard intended to sprinkle a whole cup of currants between each layer of bread. Rather the one cup was to be divided among the layers. The result is firm pudding, more like baked French toast than the custard version above.

6 thin slices of firm white bread
Butter
1 cup currants soaked in
　1/2 cup hot water
3 eggs
3 cups of milk
1/2 cup sugar, brown or white
1/2 teaspoon cinnamon
1/4 teaspoon freshly grated nutmeg

Preheat oven to 325°. Butter both sides of the bread and place the whole slices in a greased 9" x 13" baking dish with currants sprinkled between the layers of bread. Beat the eggs and add the milk, sugar, salt, and spices and beat all together. Pour the mixture over the bread. Let stand for a half hour before baking it for 35 minutes. Serve warm or cold.

Serves 4-6

APPLE DUMPLINGS

Apple Dumpling, No. 2.

Select large, fair, pleasant sour, and mellow apples; pare them, and take out the core with a small knife, and fill up the place with sugar; prepare some pie-crust, roll it out quite thick, and cut it into pieces just large enough to cover one apple. Lay an apple on each piece, and enclose them entirely; tie them up in a thick piece of cloth that has been well floured, put them in a pot of boiling water, and boil them one hour; if the boiling should stop they will be heavy. Serve them up with sweet sauce, or butter and sugar.

From *New England Economical Housekeeper*, by Mrs. E.A. Howland, 1845

MOST MODERN RECIPES for apple dumplings call for the crust-encased apples to be baked. The truth of the matter is that to twentieth-century people boiled apple dumplings are heavy even if they don't stop boiling. They are good-tasting either way: if you want an authentic apple dumpling, boil it; if you don't care, bake it.

Use your favorite pie-crust recipe (or the one on page 172), and a cooking apple like a Cortland, Baldwin, or even a Granny Smith. Serve with the traditional butter and sugar, or a sweet sauce, or just heavy cream.

Apples
   (as many as there are to be servings)
Brown sugar
Pie crust (a two-crust recipe will wrap
   up 6 medium apples)
Cinnamon or nutmeg (optional)

Preheat oven to 350° or set a large kettle-ful of water on to boil. Core and, if you wish, pare your apples. Fill the centers with brown sugar and sprinkle in a bit of spice if you wish. Divide the pie dough into as many equal-sized pieces as need-ed for the number of apples you have. Roll the crust out a quarter of an inch thick. Set the apple into the center and wrap the crust up around it.

If boiling apples: Smooth the dough up and all around the apples. Make sure your boiling cloth or bag is thoroughly wet with hot water, and flour it gener-ously. Tie the apples up in the cloth separately and tightly. Put into the pot. Boil for an hour, making sure they are floating and boiling the whole time. Add a hot teakettle full of water, if necessary. When done, cut through the ties, and put the dumplings into individual serving dishes. Cut them open and serve with butter and sugar.

If baking apples: Pinch the dough shut around each apple, making the crust a bit decorative if you wish. Set in a baking pan and bake for about an hour, or until the crust is golden. Serve warm.

WHORTLEBERRY POT PIE

Whortleberry-Pie.—Pick over the berries, and, if bought of berry-boys, or in the market, wash and dry them; but if you can trust the hands that gathered them, rubbing them gently in a coarse cloth is the best way, as you lose none of the flavor. Fill a deep plate, after having rolled the berries in sugar, and cover quite thick with sugar after they are put on the plate. No spice. Bake with upper and under crust. Some add a few currants to whortleberries, or a little juice of lemon, but we think nothing can improve their natural flavor.

From *All Around the House; or, How to Make Homes Happy*,
by Mrs. H.W. Beecher, 1878

ABOARD THE WHALING BARK *Ohio*, Fred and Sallie Smith, or their steward, combined a standard fruit pie recipe and the typical pot pie of the period, which had a dumpling-like crust, to make a whortleberry pot pie. I have not yet found a printed or manuscript recipe for a fruit-filled pot pie by that name; usually they were made with meat or poultry. Today we would call this dish a "cobbler" or a "grunt" and we prefer a baked topping over a steamed one.

Whortleberries are not hard to find in the store these days, especially when you understand that the term was used in New England in the nineteenth century for what we call blueberries. If you buy them fresh, you are still well advised to wash them, though not for the same reason mentioned by Mrs. Beecher. In her earlier cookbook, Miss Hall took a different tack from Mrs. Beecher about the matter of spice, instructing cooks to grate in nutmeg,

and also dredge in flour to thicken the pie. Certainly the filling in a slice of Mrs. Beecher's pie would have run out all over the plate.

This recipe gives you two options in the final steps. If you decide to bake it, your top will be like shortcake, and you can serve it upside down or spooned into bowls. If you decide to steam it, you will have a dumpling like top. Either way, it is delicious with whipped cream or ice cream.

2 cups blueberries
2 tablespoons sugar, or more to taste
A grating of nutmeg or to taste
A tablespoon of instant tapioca
1 cup of flour
1-1/4 teaspoon of cream of tartar
1/2 teaspoon baking soda
2 tablespoons of sugar
1/4 teaspoon salt
2 tablespoons of butter
1/3 cup of milk

Mix the blueberries, sugar, nutmeg, and tapioca together and put into a deep baking dish with a lid. Whisk together the dry ingredients, and cut in the butter. Add the milk and toss the ingredients until a ball of dough forms. Turn out onto a lightly floured board, and pat out to about half an inch thick, lift gently and put on top of the blueberries.

To bake it: Set the baking dish, uncovered into a 375° oven for 30 minutes or until the biscuit topping is browned.

To steam it: Set the dish into a larger pot with enough boiling water in it to come part-way up the sides of the saucepan, but not so much that the pan floats. Cover it with a tight-fitting lid. Steam for 30 minutes, adding more water as needed from a hot kettle.

Serve with whipped cream.

Yields 4 servings.

ORANGE JELLY

Ingredients: Eight oranges, two lemons, three-quarters of a box of gelatin soaked in half a pint of cold water, three-quarters of a pound of loaf-sugar, one pint of boiling water, beaten whites and shells of two eggs. Rub the loaf-sugar on the peels of two oranges and one lemon; squeeze the juice from six or seven oranges and two lemons, and strain it. Take off the peel carefully from two oranges, leaving only the transparent skin surrounding the quarters, and separate all the sections without breaking them. Soak the gelatin half an hour in half a pint of water; boil the other pint of water and sugar together, skimming all the time till no more scum rises; then put in the sections of oranges, and when they have boiled about a minute take them out, and put them one side. Pour this sirup [sic] over the soaked gelatin, adding the orange and lemon juice, the beaten whites and the shells of two eggs. Put it on the fire, and let it boil about a quarter of a minute without stirring; then place it at the side of the fire, skim off carefully all the scum at the top, and pass it through the jelly-bag. When half the jelly is in the mold, put it on the ice, and let it set hard enough to hold the orange sections, which place in a circular row around the edge of the mold; then add enough more jelly to cover the sections; when this has hardened, pour over the remainder of the jelly, which should have been kept in a warm place to prevent it from hardening. All the sections of orange may be put in with the first half of the jelly, as they will rise to the top, although they will not hold their places evenly. Or, if time is valuable, mold the jelly without the sections, and save them to garnish the jelly on the dish.

From *Practical Cooking and Dinner Giving,* by Mrs. Mary F. Henderson, 1882

THIS DELICATE, LIGHT DESSERT has a notably better flavor than its modern instant counterpart. Besides its wonderful flavor, it has a simply beautiful color. But little wonder that instant gelatin desserts were developed in the late 1800s. In the early nineteenth century and before, jellies were very fashionable and were served on special occasions. Gelatin for a statuesque jelly presented at dinner was extracted from calves feet by an involved process that was a sign of ample kitchen help. Isinglass extracted from fish was also available for jelly-making; but commercially prepared gelatin, similar to the sort we have today, finally simplified jelly-making for ordinary households in the last quarter of the nineteenth century.

I have taken the liberty of simplifying the old recipe. The egg whites and shells have been banished (their function was to settle impurities from the gelatin and sugar, no longer a problem). I have substituted the straining through a jelly bag with running the mixture through cheesecloth. You could substitute juice made from a concentrate if you wanted to; you will need about 3-1/2 cups. But it won't taste as good as freshly squeezed juice.

8 juice oranges
2 lemons
3-3/4 tablespoons unflavored gelatin
1 cup cold water
1-1/2 cups sugar
2 cups boiling water

Squeeze juice from seven oranges and two lemons; strain through a sieve to remove pulp. Set aside. Peel the remaining orange to use for garnishing. Dissolve the gelatin in a large pan with the cup of cold water. Meanwhile, boil the sugar and two cups of water together in another pan. When the syrup comes to boil, dip the orange sections in it briefly, using a slotted spoon, then set them aside. Pour the syrup into the gelatin, add the juice, and bring to a boil together, then immediately take it off the heat.

Wet your mold with cold water, or oil it. Lay a piece of cheese cloth in a wire strainer, and strain the jelly mixture through it into the mold. If you use the orange sections in the jelly, fill the molds half full and place in the refrigerator to partly set up. Keep the remaining jelly just at a liquid point by warming it slightly.

When the refrigerated jelly has set up enough to hold the orange sections, lay the sections in the jelly then pour the remaining jelly through the cheesecloth and sieve into the mold. Return to the refrigerator to chill thoroughly.

To serve, remove from the mold by warming a towel repeatedly with hot water, and holding it on the mold inverted on a serving plate until the jelly comes free. Garnish with more orange sections, or orange and lemon zest.

Yields a 1-1/2-quart jelly.

STRAWBERRY SHORTCAKE

330. STRAWBERRY SHORTCAKE.—

Into three pints of flour rub dry two heaping teaspoonfuls of cream of tartar, add one half cup of butter, a little salt, one teaspoonful of soda dissolved in a pint of milk and water, mix thoroughly and quickly, roll to an inch in thickness, and bake twenty minutes in a quick oven. When done divide it and cover with strawberries and sugar, to be eaten while warm.

From *The Handy Home Book,* by William M. Cornell, M.D., 1875

THIS IS A BISCUIT-TYPE shortcake. The old recipe makes a large cake so I have divided the recipe in thirds to produce a family-sized shortcake.

2 cups flour
3/4 teaspoon cream of tartar
1/2 teaspoon baking soda
1/2 teaspoon salt
1-1/3 tablespoon butter
2/3 cup milk
1 quart of ripe strawberries
Sugar

Preheat oven to 400°. Sift together dry ingredients. Cut in butter. Add the milk gradually, mixing thoroughly and quickly. Roll or pat out to an inch thick and bake on a greased sheet for 20 minutes. Slice the strawberries and add sugar, toss, and allow to sit and form a juice. Taste, and add more sugar if needed.

When the shortcake is baked, divide it and cover with strawberries and sugar to taste. Eat warm with whipped cream.

Serves 6-8.

STRAWBERRY SHORTCAKE
WITH CREAM

1 cup of powdered sugar, creamed with one tablespoonful of butter
3 eggs
1 cup of prepared flour, heaping.
2 tablespoonfuls of cream.

Beat the yolks into the creamed butter and sugar; the cream, then the whites, alternately with the flour. Bake in three jelly-cake tins. When cold, lay between the cakes nearly a quart of fresh, ripe strawberries. Sprinkle each layer with powdered sugar, and sift the same whitely over the top. Eat fresh with cream poured upon each slice.

From *The Dinner Year Book,* by Marion Harland, 1878

THIS SPONGE-CAKE type of shortcake tastes like lady-fingers. The biggest difference between Mrs. Harland's recipe and modern strawberry shortcake lies in how the cream is served—poured over, instead of whipped.

If you have "jelly tins"—small-diameter baking tins—you may want to try making a triple-layer shortcake. The following recipe will yield two 8-inch cakes. To make powdered sugar, put granulated sugar into a blender or food processor for a few moments at a high speed. "Prepared flour" is self-rising flour; or you may use all-purpose flour and add a teaspoon of baking powder to each cup of flour.

1 cup powdered sugar
3 eggs, separated
1 cup self-rising flour
or 1 cup flour plus 1 teaspoon baking powder
2 tablespoons cream
1 quart sliced strawberries
Powdered sugar

Preheat oven to 350°. Cream together butter and sugar. Beat yolks and add to butter and sugar. Add the flour, and cream alternately. Beat the whites until stiff but not dry. Gently fold in the beaten whites. Divide the batter between two greased and wax-paper-lined 8-inch pans or among three 6-inch pans. Bake for 20 minutes. Turn cakes out of pans and cool.

Just before serving, layer in the strawberries, sprinkling on sugar to taste, ending with strawberries on top, and pouring cream over, or serving it in a pitcher at the table for each to add to taste.

Serves 4-6.

CHOCOLATE ICE CREAM

Chocolate Ice Cream is made the same way as the vanilla ice-cream, adding a flavoring of chocolate and a little vanilla powder. For instance, to make a quart and a half of cream: Make the boiled custard with the yolks of six eggs, half a pound of sugar, one pint of boiled milk, and a tea-spoonful (not heaping) of vanilla powder. Pound smooth four ounces of chocolate; add a little sugar and one or two table-spoonfuls of hot water. Stir it over the fire until it is perfectly smooth. Add this and a tablespoonful of thin, dissolved gelatin to the hot custard. When about to set in the freezer, add one pint of cream, whipped.

From *Practical Cooking and Dinner Giving*, by Mrs. Mary F. Henderson, 1882

AFTER VANILLA-AND FRUIT-FLAVORED ice creams and ices, chocolate appears as a popular flavor in nineteenth-century sources. Chocolate came in several forms, including "sticks," bars, and cakes that apparently varied, as they do today, in richness and sweetness. You can find vanilla powder in some grocery stores, or in specialty food shops. Try to make the custard for the ice cream a day before you plan to freeze it to allow it to chill overnight. This recipe is a personal favorite and the one I make for birthdays and special occasions.

2 cups milk

1 cup sugar

6 egg yolks

4 ounces unsweetened chocolate

2 teaspoons vanilla extract

**1 teaspoon gelatin dissolved
   in 2 tablespoons hot water**

2 cups cream

Scald the milk in a double boiler or heavy saucepan and add the chocolate to melt it. Remove from heat. Dissolve the sugar in the milk. Beat the egg yolks and add a bit of the hot milk to them, stirring to blend, then gradually add that mixture to the rest of the scalded milk. Add the dissolved gelatin to the hot milk, and cook over hot water until thickened as for custard. Add the vanilla. Chill the custard.

When you are ready to freeze the ice cream, whip the cream until it holds a soft peak and fold it into the chilled custard. Pour into the freezer and churn, following the instructions for using your freezer, until the ice cream is frozen. Eat immediately or repack to freeze harder for later.

Yields one half-gallon.

PEACH ICE CREAM

1 quart of rich milk and as much sweet cream; 4 cups of sugar; 6 eggs; 1 quart of very ripe peaches pared and cut small....

Heat the milk; pour it upon the eggs and sugar. Cook, stirring steadily fifteen minutes, or until it has thickened well. When perfectly cold, add the cream. ... stir in the peaches just before closing the freezer for the second time, beating them well into the congealing cream. Unless they are very sweet, you would do well to dredge them in sugar before they go in.

From *The Dinner Yearbook,* by Marion Harland, 1878

"WITH A PATENT FIVE-MINUTE freezer (it really takes, however, from fifteen minutes to half an hour to freeze anything), it is as cheap and easy to make ices in summer as almost any other kind of dessert," said Mrs. Henderson in the introduction to her "Ices" recipes. A half hour of slow, steady ice-cream cranking, even speeded up by improved ice-cream freezers, was something nineteenth-century New Englanders hoped to cut short. The Victorian love of a highly molded and decorated dessert included ice cream as well. Putting the frozen ice cream into a mold, or putting two or three different flavors together in a block that could be trimmed with nuts or circled with whipped cream, took effort and had to be eaten quickly in the summer. Ice cream served at a picnic was probably served less formally, scooped directly from the freezer container onto cake-laden plates.

Whipping or light cream are good choices for "sweet cream." You can make this as rich as you like.

1 quart whole milk or half-and-half, or a blend of the two
4 cups sugar
6 eggs
1 quart cream
1 quart peeled and crushed, fully ripe peaches, sweetened to taste

Scald the milk in a double boiler. Beat together eggs and sugar; when the milk is hot, pour it into the egg mixture gradually and blend, return to the double boiler and cook till it has thickened and coats the back of a spoon.

Chill. (If you keep it in the refrigerator overnight and freeze it the next day; it will make a better ice cream.) When you are ready to freeze the ice cream, whip the cream and fold it into the custard. Pour into the freezer.

Following the instructions for using your freezer, churn the ice cream until it is thick enough for you to feel resistance as you turn the crank. At this point, remove the top and add the peaches. Continue churning till the ice cream is frozen. Eat immediately or repack to freeze harder for later.

Yields 3 quarts.

LEMON ICE CREAM

Three cupfuls of sugar, the juice of three lemons, three pints cream, the yolks of eight eggs, one pint water. Boil the water, sugar, and lemon juice together twenty mints; then proceed as for vanilla ice cream...

... Beat the yolks of the eggs with one-fourth teaspoon of salt. Place the basin of boiling syrup in another of boiling water. Stir the yolks ... into the syrup and beat rapidly for three minutes. Take the basin from the fire, place it in a pan of ice water and beat until cold. Add cream and freeze.

From *Miss Parloa's New Cook Book*, by Maria Parloa, 1880

THIS RECIPE MAKES a delicately flavored lemon ice cream. If you prefer a more lemony flavor, put in more juice or add the grated rind of one or two lemons. You can vary the richness of the ice cream by using either light, whipping, or heavy cream.

3 cups sugar
Juice of three lemons
2 cups of water
8 egg yolks
1/4 teaspoon salt
6 cups cream

In a heavy saucepan, boil together sugar, lemon juice, and water for about 20 minutes. Put into the top of a double boiler in boiling water. Beat the egg yolks and salt together, and then using a whisk or electric beater add to the hot syrup, beating constantly for three minutes. Put the top of the boiler into a pan of cold water, and beat the yolks and syrup until it is cold. You may wish to change the water in the pan to cool it down again. Whisk in the cream and pour into the freezer.

Following the instructions for using your freezer, churn the ice cream until it is frozen. Eat immediately or repack to freeze harder for later.

Yields slightly more than a gallon.

RICE MERINGUE

One half cup of Rice cooked in one quart of milk, 4 eggs, two cups sugar – one good lemon. When the Rice is cooked add the yolks of the eggs, two tablespoons of the Sugar, the grated peel of the lemon, a little salt, Stir all together and bake, then let it cool. Take the white of the eggs – The rest of the Sugar, and the juice of the lemon, beat it to a perfect froth. When your pudding is cool pour it over and let it bake a few minutes until a light brown.

From the manuscript receipt book, ca. 1844-1880 of Mary E. B. Fish. James D. Fish Family Papers, Coll. 211, G.W. Blunt-White Library, Mystic Seaport

---

IN MARY FISH'S time this was a fashionable and stylish presentation, and one of several elegant desserts she included in her manuscript recipe notebook. She and her Mystic native husband James lived in New York City where maritime trade business took them. It may remind you of the meringue topped Queen of Puddings on page 124. Topping a homely bread or rice pudding with meringue really dressed up the dish and made it suitable for company.

The recipe calls for four eggs, which in the nineteenth century were somewhat smaller than the average large egg of today. Three will do.

1 quart of milk
1/2 cup rice
3 large eggs, separated
2 tablespoons of sugar
Grated peel of one lemon
3 egg whites
3 tablespoons sugar
2 tablespoons of lemon juice

Heat the milk and rice in a double boiler over hot water for 30 to 35 minutes or until the rice is tender. Preheat the oven to 325°. Bring water to a boil in a tea kettle for a hot-water bath to bake the pudding in. Butter a 1-1/2 quart baking dish. In a separate small bowl, lightly beat the egg yolks and spoon half a cup of the hot milk into them, mixing well. Add the beaten yolks and milk to the rice and milk mixture, with the sugar and lemon peels. Mix thoroughly and take off the heat. Pour it into the buttered baking dish, and set the dish into a baking pan. Put into the oven and add hot water until it comes about a third to halfway up the side of the pudding dish. Bake for half an hour, or until a knife inserted comes out clean.

Remove from the oven and allow to cool slightly.

Beat egg whites until frothy then add the lemon juice and sugar gradually, beating constantly. When the meringue makes soft peaks, spread it on the cooled pudding and put it into a 350° oven for 10 to 15 minutes or until it is a delicate golden color.

Serves six.

8 Cakes and Cookies

CAKES AND COOKIES WERE UTTERLY TRANSFORMED over the course of the nineteenth century. At the start of the 1800s, cake meant a dough made with eggs and butter, and enriched with fruit and spices, and raised by yeast. Within a couple of decades chemical leavens were in common use, the earliest one called pearlash, an alkaline product made from refined potash, which interacted with an acid ingredient such as milk, molasses or lemon juice. It was replaced quickly by a carbonate of soda called saleratus and eventually by bicarbonate of soda also an alkaline often used in conjunction with the acid cream of tartar. By the end of the century baking powders which mixed the alkaline and acid ingredients in one were common, and those were sometimes mixed with flour to make self-rising flour.

At the start of the 1800s, the word cookie had migrated from the Dutch in New York into New England but most people making cookie-like baked goods, called them "cakes" plural, many recipes for which can be found in early cookbooks. These labor intensive pastries were most common among the wealthier classes who had kitchen help, and could afford to heat their ovens continuously to accomplish the baking. When cook stoves became more common, heating an oven quickly was more simply done, and more cookies were made in ordinary homes. By the early 1900s, many more cookie recipes appeared in cookbooks.

If you decide to make cookies in your fireplace oven you will replicate the early experience of the oven cooling off as you more frequently open and close the oven to put the cookies in and take them out. You will want to maintain a brisk fire in the fireplace to create new coals so that you can reheat the oven with shovels full of new coals. You may wish to keep a ring of embers at the back and side edges of the oven taking care to keep the cookie-laden baking sheet away from them to avoid scorching.

POUND CAKE

Modern recipes for pound cake measure the ingredients in cups, obscuring the reason for the name "pound" cake, which used to contain one pound each of butter, sugar, flour and eggs. If you have a kitchen scale you are much better off weighing the ingredients because amounts of flour measured in cups may vary quite a bit. I like nutmeg for spice in pound cake, but in the early days brandy, mace, and rosewater were used, too. Sometimes caraway seed was added. This recipe yields two standard-sized loaves of cake. You can also bake it in a bundt or tube pan. This recipe can easily be cut to create a "half-pound" cake.

TO BAKE THIS IN A fireplace oven, plan to put it in after the initial heat of the oven has declined, and have the sugar, flour, and butter mixed together so you are ready to add the eggs at the last minute before putting the cake in the oven.

1 pound or 2 cups butter
1 pound of 2-1/2 cups sugar
1 pound or 8 large eggs
1 pound or 4 cups flour

Flavoring to taste:
2 tablespoons brandy
1 teaspoon nutmeg, mace or cinnamon
2-3 tablespoons of rosewater

Preheat oven to 300° and grease two loaf pans or a tube pan. Rub the butter, sugar, and flour together. Beat the eggs lightly and add the flour and sugar mixture. Mix in the spice and brandy or rosewater, and beat until you have a smooth batter. Bake one hour and fifteen minutes or until a tester inserted comes out clean.

Yields two loaves.

SPONGE CAKE

Eight eggs balance 6 with sugar four with flour: half a glass of brandy-one nutmeg.

From the manuscript recipe notebook of Julia Palmer, ca. 1840-60

SPONGE CAKE, besides being a very nice cake to serve at tea, formed the basis for the popular nineteenth-century desserts Charlotte Russe and Trifle. Classic sponge cake recipes were written with ingredients measured by their weight in eggs, as is Miss Palmer's recipe above but by the end of the nineteenth century, sponge cake recipes were usually written down in measures. Another change was from leavening the cake entirely with beaten egg white to the use of chemical leavens like cream of tartar and baking soda, or baking powder. Brandy was the more common flavoring in pre-Temperance-era New England but was edged out by lemon flavoring in the last half of the century. Lemon and orange flavorings are popular today but you might enjoy using nutmeg instead, at least one teaspoon, plus a couple of tablespoons of brandy.

The eggs in Julia Palmer's time were small by today's standard, so in the recipe that follows I have made an adjustment for conventional large eggs. If you wish to have an experience of early cake making practice, try weighing out the sugar and flour in the proportions suggested by the old recipe using six large eggs. It is actually more difficult to get this cake right using cup measurements.

If you bake this cake in a fireplace oven, remember that you will have to beat and fold in the egg whites and the flour just before you put the cake in the oven; allow yourself ten minutes at least.

6 large eggs (about 13 ounces)
1-1/4 cups sugar (9.75 ounces)
1 lemon, rind and juice
1-1/2 cups flour (6.5 ounces)

Preheat oven to 350°. Grease and flour an 8-inch tube pan. Separate the eggs, and beat the yolks till light and lemon-colored. Add the sugar and continue to beat well, till the mixture holds its shape briefly when dropped from a spoon. Add lemon juice and rind. In separate bowl, beat the whites until stiff, but not dry; a pinch of cream of tartar helps the eggs stay firm. Fold into the yolks and sugar.

Last, sprinkle the flour a little at a time onto the batter and fold gently and lightly into the mixture. Spoon into the baking pan. Bake for one hour, or until it pulls away from the sides of the pan and is firm to the touch. Allow to cool and remove from the pan. Shake confectioner's sugar over the top of the cake, or serve with a fruit compote.

Yields one 8-inch tube cake.

ELECTION CAKE

Four pounds of flour, three quarters of a pound of butter, four eggs, one pound of sugar, half a pint of good yeast, wet with milk as stiff as can be molded on a board. Set to rise overnight in winter; in warm weather three hours is usually enough to rise. Bake about three quarters of an hour.

From *New England Economical Housekeeper*, by Mrs. E.A. Howland, 1845

BEFORE THE 1800s cakes were essentially sweetened bread raised by yeast or by egg, sometimes enriched by spices and fruit like nutmeg, mace, wine, brandy, and raisins. Election Cake was customarily made in southern New England households anticipating an influx of company as country people came in to town to vote, hence the generous proportions of this cake.

If you bake this in a fireplace oven, bear in mind that you will want to time it so that the yeasted dough has had adequate time to rise.

**2 teaspoons dry yeast dissolved
   in 1/2 cup of warm water**
3-1/2 cups flour
Generous 1/2 cup sugar
1 teaspoon nutmeg
5 tablespoons butter
1 egg
Scant 1/2 cup milk
1/2 cup raisins soaked in 1/4 cup brandy

Grease and flour a ten-inch tube pan. Dissolve the yeast in the water and set aside. Mix together the flour, sugar and spices, and rub the butter into them until it is entirely incorporated. Beat the egg and add to the milk, and add both to the yeast. Beat the liquids into the flour to form a dough. Add the raisins and brandy. If necessary, add just enough flour to knead the dough, but let it remain somewhat sticky. Knead an additional 15 or 20 times. Fit the dough into the pan and allow to rise 2 to 2-1/2 hours or until double in size. Preheat oven to 350°.

Bake for 35 to 40 minutes. Cool on a rack. If you wish, you can make an icing of confectioners sugar and milk to drizzle over the cake when it is cool.

WEDDING CAKE

Four pounds of flour, three
pounds of Sugar, three pounds
of Butter four pounds of
currants, thirty eggs, half
a pint of molasses, one
gill of wine, one gill of
Brandy & Spice.

From the manuscript recipe notebook of Mary Miller, ca 1850-1870, in a private collection

BRIDE'S CAKE

Beat to a cream one pound of butter and one pound of fine white sugar; then add a quarter of a pound of sifted flour, and three eggs well beaten; mix this well together; then stir in another quarter of a pound of sifted flour, then three eggs well beaten; mix this well, then stir in half a gill of prime brandy, quarter of an ounce of mace, one teaspoonful of cinnamon, quarter of a pound of Muscatel raisins stoned and cut in halves, two ounces of citron, two of candied orange peel, two of candied lemon peel, all cut in slips; stir all well together, and add two eggs well beaten; mix a quarter of a pound of sifted flour with one and half pounds of Zante currants picked, washed and dried; stir the currants into the cake; mix the whole well, and bake two hours in a buttered hoop lined with double paper. If the bottom of the cake browns too fast in the oven, slip a board under it; when done, turn the cake upside down and ice it all over, ...

To Ice a Cake.
Dredge that side of the cake which rested upon the tin while baking, with sifted flour, in order to remove whatever grease there may be there; then wipe off the flour carefully, put a quantity of icing in the centre, and with a broad-bladed knife spread it equally over the top and over the other sides of the cake, dipping your knife occasionally in cold water as you proceed; then put the cake in a warm oven, that the icing may harden, but not allowing it to remain in the oven long enough to discolor the icing. If you wish to ornament this icing, trail icing upon it, in whatever forms you choose, through a tin or paper tube; or adorn it with sugar plums, or other confectionary, before you harden it in the oven.

Both recipes above from *The Practical Cookbook,* by Mrs. Bliss, 1864

Wedding cake or Bride's cake was a customary refreshment at wedding celebrations in the nineteenth century. The traditional wedding cake was a fruit cake which helps explain why the very top layer was set aside for the newly-weds to enjoy a year later.

Mrs. Bliss devoted a whole chapter to "Ornaments for Cakes," providing recipes for icing and sugar trims. Most icings, as you may have noticed, are not butter frostings, but are made from varying proportions of beaten egg whites and sugar. Besides icing in fancy shapes, Mrs. Bliss describes how to make colored sugar, using spinach essence, cochineal, indigo, saffron, and other sources of color. Bits of jelly could be added for decoration as well as sugar-plums, which were essentially candied fruits.

GOLD CAKE AND SILVER CAKE

Silver Cake—nice.

One cup sugar, half cup butter, one-fourth teaspoon soda dissolved in a half teacup milk, whites 5 eggs, three-fourth teaspoon cream of tartar mixed in two cups of flour. Yolks of the eggs and the same ingredients make gold cake.

From *Mrs. Winslow's Domestic Receipt Book for 1871*

GOLD AND SILVER CAKES are complementary: the yolks of eggs are used in one and the whites are used in the other. They became fashionable in the last quarter of the 1800s, and often appear on the same page in printed cookbooks and in manuscript books, too.

GOLD CAKE

2 cups flour
1 teaspoon cream of tartar
1/2 teaspoon baking soda
1 cup sugar
2/3 cup butter
4 egg yolks
3/4 cup milk
1 teaspoon lemon or vanilla extract

Preheat oven to 350°. Grease and flour two 8-inch pans. Sift together dry ingredients. Cream together butter and sugar using an electric mixer if you wish. Beat egg yolks till lemony and beat in the butter and sugar. Add extract.

Add dry ingredients to the wet ingredients alternately with the milk. The batter will be stiff. Divide into the two baking pans, and bake for 20 to 25 minutes, or until a tester inserted comes out clean, and the cake pulls away from the sides of the pan. Cool and remove from pans. Frost with any frosting you like.

Yields two 8-inch-diameter cakes.

SILVER CAKE

2-1/2 cups flour
1 teaspoon cream of tartar
1/2 teaspoon baking soda
2 cups sugar
1/2 cup butter
3/4 cup milk
4 egg whites
1 teaspoon vanilla or almond extract

Preheat oven to 350°. Grease and flour two 8-inch pans. Sift together dry ingredients. Cream together butter and sugar using an electric mixer if you wish. In a separate bowl, beat the whites till they form stiff peaks. Add dry ingredients to the wet ingredients alternately with the milk. Fold in the egg whites. Divide into the two baking pans, and bake for 35 minutes, or until a tester inserted comes out clean, and the cake pulls away from the sides of the pan. Cool and remove from pans. Frost with any frosting you like.

Yields two 8-inch-diameter cakes.

COCONUT CAKE

1.2.3.4.Cocoanut Cake
1 cup butter
2 cups sugar
3 cups flour
4 eggs whites only
1 cup milk
1 teaspoon cream of tartar
1/2 teaspoon soda
1 small cocoanut

From the manuscript recipe notebook of Julia Gates, 1857-1930 in the collection of the Mystic River Historical Society

COCONUT CAKE was "a prominent kind of cake" in the last quarter of the nineteenth century and early twentieth century, especially for picnics, according to the recollections of a woman from an old North Stonington family. This version, based on the old "One, two, three, four cake" gets its name from the recipe content: 1 cup butter, 2 cups sugar, etc., and early in the century it was also called cup cake because the measuring was all in cups. It is moist, rich and absolutely delicious.

Using freshly grated coconut is the best way to make this cake. With a food processor or a super-sharp hand grater, it is not as much trouble as it was for earlier cooks. If you use sweetened coconut, you may need to reduce the amount of sugar by a couple tablespoons. One average-sized coconut gave me about five cups grated coconut, which was enough for the cake and frosting.

The leftover yolks from making this cake and a boiling frosting for it, will give you the six yolks you need for the chocolate ice cream on page 140.

1 cup butter
2 cups sugar
3 cups flour
1 teaspoon cream of tartar
1/2 teaspoon baking soda
4 egg whites
1 cup milk
2-1/2 cups grated coconut

Preheat oven to 350°. Grease two 9-inch pans and line with waxed paper. Sift together the dry ingredients and cream together the butter and sugar. Beat in the milk. Add the dry ingredients to the wet ingredients. Mix in the grated coconut. Beat the egg whites until stiff and fold them into the cake. Spoon into the baking pans.

Bake for 45 minutes, or until the cake is firm in the center, pulls away from the sides of the pan, and a tester inserted comes out clean.

FROSTING

Cocoanut icing between is nice—

1 grated coconut, to 1/2 of this add whites of 3 eggs beaten to a froth & 1 cup powdered sugar. Lay this between the layers. Mix with the other half of the cocoanut, 4 tablespoons sugar and strew thickly on top.

From the manuscript recipe notebook of Julia Gates, 1857-1930

MRS. GATES used this icing on the White Mountain cake she included in her notebook, copied from Marion Harland's *Dinner Year Book* published in 1878. My personal favorite icing for coconut cake is a modern Seven Minute Boiled icing, found in most standard cookbooks. But I think the icing above is good with coconut cake and will give you a taste of the past.

FILLING

3 egg whites
1 cup confectioner's sugar
1 cup of grated coconut

Beat the egg whites until frothy and continue beating gradually adding the sugar, until it is all incorporated. Fold in the coconut, and spread between the layers of the cake.

TOPPING

1/4 cup granulated sugar
1-1/2 cups of grated coconut

Toss together and spread thickly on top of the cake.

Yields enough filling and icing for one cake.

SOFT GINGERBREAD

One cup of molasses, one cup of warm water, one teaspoon of ginger, one teaspoon saleratus, four tablespoons of melted butter Stir flour in very thin. Use top of the pot or pork fat for shortening.

From logbook of schooner *William B. Herrick*, 1874-76, Log 713, G.W. Blunt White Library, Mystic Seaport Museum

THERE WERE TWO BASIC TYPES of gingerbread in the nineteenth century. One was a soft cake-like gingerbread made with molasses, and called either soft or molasses gingerbread. The other was a hard, cookie-like gingerbread made with sugar and called hard or sugar gingerbread. This soft gingerbread from the logbook of the *Herrick* is typical of the soft gingerbreads, but is made with water instead of milk and without eggs. The note about alternative shortenings is particularly interesting: ashore, butter was easy to come by. At sea, a ready and cheap source of shortening could be lard, pork fat (from fried pork or even bacon), or fat from boiled meat, which would rise to the top of the pot, congeal when cold, and could be skimmed off. The molasses would overwhelm the stronger flavor of the meat fats.

This gingerbread is a nice moist one with a rich flavor and a crusty top when fresh out of the oven.

2 cups flour
1 teaspoon of ginger
1 teaspoon baking soda
4 tablespoons of melted butter or lard
1 cup molasses
1 cup of warm water

Preheat oven to 350°. Grease an 8" x 8" pan. Sift together the dry ingredients. Melt the butter, add the molasses and warm water (from the tap), and mix well. Add gradually to the dry ingredients, blending well. Pour into the baking pan and bake for 30 minutes, or until the top cracks slightly and a tester inserted comes out clean.

Yields one 8 x 8-inch gingerbread.

RAILROAD CAKE

1 cup of Sugar
3 Eggs
3 tablespoonful of melted butter
1 tea " " Cream tartar
1/2 " " " Soda
1 cup of flour
Flavor to taste

From the manuscript recipe notebook of Fannie Card, Westerly, Rhode Island, 1879

RAILROAD CAKE, like delicate cake, was a locally popular dessert. Fannie Card had no fewer than three railroad cake recipes in her receipt book, and Julia Gates included it in hers as well. One of the three Card recipes recommends "Bake in 3 or 4 thin layers while warm spread with jelly, frost the top layer." Another recipe, from the second decade of the nineteenth century, recommends a chocolate frosting.

1 cup flour
1 teaspoon cream of tartar
1 teaspoon baking soda
3 tablespoons melted butter
1 cup sugar
3 eggs
1 cup jelly or jam, any flavor

Preheat oven to 350°. Grease two round 8" pans and line with waxed paper. Sift together dry ingredients. Beat together sugar and eggs till the mixture is very thick and creamy, and creates soft peaks. Fold in the dry ingredients, and blend in the melted butter. Divide the batter in the two pans, and bake 25 minutes until the center is firm when touched with a finger and a tester inserted comes out clean. Remove from pans and spread with jelly while cakes are still warm. Frost with your choice of icing.

Yields two 8" cakes.

FRUITCAKE AND FROSTING

Fruit cake

two lbs sifted flour
" " loaf sugar
" " butter
" " raisins
1 lb citron
1 " almonds
18 eggs
1 teacup brandy
a little soda
All kinds of spice

From manuscript recipes in the journal of Sallie Smith's voyage in the bark *Ohio*, 1876-77, manuscript collection, G.W. Blunt White Library, Mystic Seaport Museum

SOME SEAFARERS TOOK fruitcake with them to enjoy at sea; Mrs. Smith took her recipe, or perhaps collected it from another whaling wife and penciled it in the back of her journal along with a number of other recipes. Nineteenth-century fruitcake recipe ingredients often varied. While Mrs. Smith's recipe does not include currants, a good many recipes from the same period did. Cinnamon, nutmeg, and mace are the most common spices.

This recipe yields a large amount of fruitcake, about sixteen pounds. You may wish to divide it. To help you calculate what pan sizes to use, you will find a 4-1/2" x 8-1/2" pan will yield a 2-1/2 pound cake.

9 cups sifted flour
2 teaspoons baking soda
1 tablespoon cinnamon
1-1/2 teaspoons nutmeg
1 teaspoon mace
Allspice and ginger to taste
4 cups sugar
4 cups butter
1/2 cup brandy
18 eggs
5-1/2 cups raisins
2-2/3 cups citron
5-2/3 cups slivered almonds

Preheat oven to 275°. Grease and/or line baking pans with parchment or waxed paper. Sift together dry ingredients. Cream together butter and sugar. Beat the eggs well and mix into the butter and sugar, and add the brandy. Beat in the dry ingredients. Stir in the fruit and nuts. Divide batter among your pans. Bake for 1-1/2 to 3 hours, depending on pan size, or until the cake pulls away from the side of the pan and a knife inserted comes out fairly clean.

Yields 16 pounds of fruitcake.

FROSTING

Use the white of one egg for frosting with one cup sugar, 2 tablespoonfuls cold water put the sugar and water on stove and let boil a minute, have the whites all beaten and pour the sugar in while hot, beat all together a few minutes then pour on the cake.

From the manuscript recipe notebook of Fannie Card, 1879

THIS IS A TYPICAL nineteenth-century frosting recipe. It makes enough for two layers, and is better-tasting if you add lemon or vanilla extract. It immediately follows one of Fannie Card's gold cake recipes, but would be suitable for almost any other cake recipe in this book. A word of caution, however; nineteenth-century icings are often very disappointing to twenty-first-century people. They are, to our taste, hard and flavorless. If you are interested in historical authenticity then use this recipe. If you are making a cake merely for pleasure, you may prefer one of your favorite modern frosting recipes.

The recipe is clear enough that an interpretation is not needed. Use superfine granulated sugar—or you can whirl regular granulated sugar in a blender at a high speed to make it finer.

DELICATE CAKE

2 cups Sugar.
1/2 cup Butter.
Whites of six Eggs
3/4 cup Sweet Milk.
Nearly three cups Flour.
1 teaspoonful Cream of Tartar.
1/2 " Soda.
Lemon Flavor.

From the manuscript recipe notebook of Fannie Card, 1879

"DELICATE CAKE" is another cake recipe that appears often in manuscript sources from southern New England in the last quarter of the nineteenth century. This recipe typical of delicate cake; the recipes differ mainly in the number of egg whites and the amount of butter used. This recipe is identical to the one for delicate cake that appears in *Hood's Cook Book #1,* published about the same date Fannie Card commenced her receipt book.

Delicate cake is moist, rises nicely, and makes a good white layer cake. If you like to experiment, or happen to have more egg whites than the recipe calls for, go ahead and add them. You may substitute two teaspoons of baking powder for the cream of tartar and soda.

3 cups flour
1 teaspoon cream of tartar
1/2 teaspoon baking soda
2 cups sugar
1/2 cup butter
3/4 cup milk
6 egg whites
Rind of one lemon

Preheat oven to 350°. Grease two 1-1/2-inches deep, 8-inch round cake pans, and line with waxed or parchment paper. Sift together dry ingredients. Cream together butter and sugar till fluffy. In a separate bowl, beat egg whites until stiff peaks form. Add dry ingredients and milk alternately to the butter and sugar. Beat well. Fold in the egg whites. Spread into the greased cake pans, and bake at 350° for 30 minutes, or until the center is firm to the touch, and a tester inserted comes out clean. Cool on a rack and then remove from the pans.

Yields two 8-inch-diameter cakes.

ORANGE CAKE

2 eggs
1/2 teaspoon soda
1 cup sugar
1 teaspoon cream tartar, or
1 tablespoon melted butter
3 level teasp. baking powder
1/2 cup milk
1 tablespoon orange juice and
1 1/2 cup flour a little of the grated rind.

*Mix in the order given. Bake in a round shallow pan, split, and fill with orange
cream.*

*Orange Cream for Cake.—- Put in a cup the rind of half and the juice of one
orange, one tablespoon of lemon juice and fill with cold water. Strain, and put on
to boil. Add one tablespoonful of cornstarch, wet in cold water. Stir till thick, then
cook over hot water ten minutes. Beat the yolk of one egg, add two heaping table-
spoonfuls of sugar, stir into the starch, cook one minute, add one teaspoonful of
butter, and cool.*

Fill the cake with the cream, and frost with ornamental frosting ...

From *Mrs. Lincoln's Boston Cook Book*, by Mary Lincoln, 1913

THIS CAKE IS quickly made, another in the sizeable line-up of later nineteenth- and early twentieth-century cake recipes that flourished in the wake of cheaper flour and commercially produced granulated sugar, and the more easily heated wood stove ovens. You can adjust the filling to be sweeter or more tart as you wish, by increasing or decreasing the sugar. The cake itself is sweet, so a tart filling is a nice complement. I have substituted baking powder for the baking soda and cream of tartar, but you may wish to use the latter in which case, whisk them into the flour instead of the baking powder. To frost the cake, a sprinkle of confectioners sugar is just fine, or you can make a butter and sugar icing with additional orange flavoring in it.

THE CAKE

1-1/2 cups flour
3 teaspoons baking powder
2 eggs
1 cup sugar
1 tablespoon orange juice
1–1-1/2 teaspoons grated orange rind
1/2 cup milk
1 tablespoon melted butter

Preheat oven to 350° and grease and flour one 9-inch pan.

Whisk together dry ingredients. Beat the eggs until they are foamy, then beat in the sugar and add the juice and rind. Add the dry ingredients to the sugar and butter mixture alternately with the milk, starting and ending with the dry ingredients, and mixing just enough to create a smooth batter. Then fold in the melted and cooled butter. Pour into a baking pan. Bake for 25 minutes or until a tester inserted comes out clean.

Set on racks to cool; turn out, split and make the filling.

FILLING

Juice of two oranges
1 tablespoon lemon juice
Water
1 tablespoon cornstarch
Grated rind of half an orange
1 egg yolk
2 heaping tablespoons of sugar
1 teaspoon of butter

Put the orange and lemon juices into a one cup measure and fill to the one cup line with water. Whisk one tablespoon of cornstarch into the water. Put into a double boiler or in a pan set into another pan of hot water, and cook mixture together over a medium heat until it is thick and smooth, about eight minutes. Beat the egg yolk and sugar together and whisk into the starch mixture and cook another minute or two, then add the butter. Whisk well, and take it off the heat to cool before using it.

Assemble the cake.

After it has cooled, slice the cake horizontally and spread both sides generously with the filling. Put the layers together, and frost the cake as you like.

DOUGHNUTS

DOUGH NUTS, No. 1.

Two eggs, one cup of sugar, half a pint of sour milk; a little saleratus; salt and spice to your taste; a small piece of butter or cream is better, if you have it; mix the articles together one hour before you fry the cakes; mould with flour.

From *New England Economical Housekeeper*, by Mrs. E.A. Howland, 1845

MANY WHALESHIPS like the *Charles W. Morgan* offered their crew doughnuts fried in whale oil to celebrate filling their one-thousandth barrel. Some whaling wives report that the flavor was not affected at all by the whale oil. Because most nineteenth-century doughnut recipes call for milk and eggs, I have wondered how doughnuts at sea were produced. Milk was not always available. Eggs may have been, but were precious. However, doughnuts were a special treat for which the captain might allow a few eggs. A sweetened bread dough might have been fashioned into doughnuts and fried up for the crew in lieu of the kind of doughnuts produced by the recipe above. Even today we can find both yeasted, or raised doughnuts and cake-like doughnut recipes.

Many stories purport to explain how doughnuts got their holes, and each story has loyal proponents. What is true is that doughnuts did not always have holes. They were sometimes fried up in small lumps, as a dough "nut," and at other times were cut into shapes. They were always fried in deep fat, and were considered an economical sweet suitable for filling up small boys or eating for tea. Cinnamon and nutmeg seem to have been the preferred spices for doughnuts.

To succeed, doughnuts need to be a soft, barely manageable dough fried in fat hot enough to cook them without either burning or soaking up the fat as they cook. You will find it helpful to let the dough chill before cutting the doughnuts.

Frying doughnuts in a fireplace allows the greasy smoke to go up the chimney, but provide yourself with good light so that you can observe carefully the color of the doughnuts as they cook. A medium fire is better than a hotter blaze, and be flexible about moving the pot closer to or farther from the fire to maintain an even temperature.

4-4-1/2 cups flour
1 teaspoon baking soda
1/2 teaspoon cinnamon
1/2 teaspoon nutmeg
1/2 teaspoon salt
2 eggs
1 cup sugar
1 cup sour milk
2 tablespoons butter, melted
Sufficient oil or fat for frying

Sift together dry ingredients. In a separate bowl, beat eggs well, slowly adding the sugar. When light and lemony appearing, add the milk and melted butter. Mix in the sifted dry ingredients, then set the dough in the refrigerator for an hour to chill. Turn out on a well-floured board and pat out to half an inch thick. Bring the fat to 350° degrees on a thermometer. Cut into desired shape and drop into the hot fat. Do not crowd. Cook for about 2-2-1/2 minutes per side, turning them over with a fork or chop stick. When cooked, drain on paper towels.

If you wish, put sugar and cinnamon into a paper bag and shake the doughnuts in the bag till they are coated.

Yields two dozen 2-1/2 inch diameter doughnuts.

CARAWAY CAKES

Take one pound of flour, three quarters of a pound of sugar, half a pound of butter, a glass of rosewater, four eggs, a half a teacup caraway seed—the materials well rubbed together and beat up. Drop them from a spoon on tin sheets and bake twenty or thirty minutes in rather a slow oven.

From *New England Economical Housekeeper,* by Mrs. E.A. Howland, 1844

TRADITIONALLY early-nineteenth-century caraway and other seed cakes are not as sweet as modern cookies. Rosewater was a fairly frequent ingredient in many recipes and can still be obtained if you would like to try it. You can use either brown or white sugar. When made with brown sugar, the cookies take a bit longer to bake.

If you choose to bake your caraway cakes in the fireplace oven, wait until you have removed the bread, cakes, and pies, and use the somewhat lower residual temperature. If the oven is too cool to do the job, you can spike the temperature somewhat by shoveling fresh hot coals from under the fire. If you are very careful, you can arrange the coals around the perimeter of the oven and bake the seed cakes in the center.

2 cups flour
3/4 cup sugar
1 cup butter
2 eggs
1/2 cup caraway seeds
1-1/2 teaspoons rosewater or milk

Preheat the oven to 325°. Rub flour, sugar, butter together till it looks like crumbs. Beat the eggs and stir into the rubbed mixture. Then beat all together, adding the milk or rosewater. The dough should be stiff. Drop teaspoon-sized pieces of dough on greased cookie sheets. Bake for 20 minutes until golden.

Yields 48 small cookies.

SUGAR GINGERBREAD

One quart flour, one cup shortening (pork fat and butter) rubbed into the flour, one and a half cup sugar, one tablespoon ginger, one cup sweet milk, 1 teaspoon soda.

From *Mrs. Winslow's Domestic Receipt Book for 1868*

A GINGERBREAD or ginger cookie without molasses seems a little odd today, but a standard hard or "sugar" gingerbread in the nineteenth century was usually made with sugar instead of molasses; hence its name. It was mixed stiff and rolled out on a baking pan or sheet and cut into pieces after baking. I have doubled the ginger, and recommend using butter. Before baking, sprinkle the top with sugar or ginger and sugar mixed similar to cinnamon sugar.

4-1/2 cups flour
1 tablespoon (or preferably more) ginger
1 teaspoon baking soda
1 cup butter
1-1/2 cups sugar
1 cup milk

Preheat oven to 350°. Grease two cookie sheets. Sift together the dry ingredients. Using your fingers or the back of a spoon, rub together the dry ingredients and the butter. Then mix in the sugar. Add the milk and mix thoroughly; turn the dough out on a floured board and knead lightly till it forms a smooth mass.

Divide the dough and roll or pat out on the cookie sheets to about half an inch thick. Sprinkle with sugar if you wish. Bake for 25 minutes till golden brown. Cut into squares, diamonds, or rectangles while still warm.

Yields two 15- x 10-inch sheets.

GINGERSNAPS

1 cup sugar, 1/2 cup molasses,
1/2 cup melted butter–
1/2 cup water, 1/2 tablespoon soda–flour spice.

From the manuscript recipe notebook of Julia Gates, 1857-1930,
in the collection of the Mystic River Historical Society, Mystic, Connecticut

THIS IS THE PERFECT cookie for large quantities, ideal for a Christmas open house or at other times of the year to grab by the handful to eat with milk. I love to dunk these in tea. This and other period recipes for gingersnaps often did not include ginger in the ingredient list, while others include other spices in addition to ginger.

Some period recipes require boiling the butter and molasses together, which yields a crisp, brittle cookie, while others mix the ingredients cold which produces a more tender cookie. Gingersnaps should have a very stiff dough and be rolled thin. If you have time, you may wish to chill the dough before rolling it out.

3 cups flour
1 tablespoon ginger
2 teaspoons baking soda
1/2 cup butter
1 cup sugar
1/2 cup molasses
Scant 1/2 cup water

Preheat oven to 375°. Grease your cookie sheets. Sift together flour, ginger, and soda. Melt the butter; mix it with the sugar, molasses, and water and bring to a rolling boil for a couple of minutes. Gradually add this mixture to the dry ingredients, mixing well. The dough will be very stiff. On a floured surface, roll dough very thin, at least one-sixteenth of an inch. Work quickly so it will not have time to take up flour. Cut into desired shapes and bake on a greased cookie sheet for 7 minutes.

Yields 24 dozen 2-inch cookies.

JUMBLES

1/2 lb sugar
1/2 lb butter
2/4 lb flour
2 eggs

From Sallie Smith's journal of a whaling voyage aboard the bark *Ohio*, 1875-1878, Log 399, G.W. Blunt White Library, Mystic Seaport Museum

---

JUMBLES WAS THE name given to what most people today would identify as sugar cookies, and with some variation they have been around for centuries. This brief recipe was found among others written in pencil at the back of Sallie Smith's journal, but additional instructions for making them can be found in other period recipe collections.

Traditionally jumbles were ring-shaped cookies and were rolled out in sugar, though many modern cookbooks say they ought to be filled. If you want ring shaped cookies, use a doughnut cutter. If you want filled cookies, cut three-inch round cookies, put a teaspoon of filling on one round, and place a second round on top, crimping the edges with your fingers or a fork.

You can vary the spice in these cookies to suit your taste. In the first part of the nineteenth century, lemon, nutmeg, or rosewater topped the list of preferred flavorings, and later in the century vanilla was the choice. Since Mrs. Smith doesn't specify, the choice is yours.

1 cup sugar
1 cup or two sticks of butter
2-1/2 cups flour
2 eggs
Your choice of flavorings:
    1/2 teaspoon lemon extract
    1 tablespoonful of rosewater
    1/2 grated nutmeg
    1 teaspoon vanilla

Preheat oven to 325°. Grease your cookie sheets. Cream together sugar and butter, add eggs and flavoring and flour. The dough will be quite stiff. Chill the dough for an hour. Sprinkle your rolling surface with granulated sugar. Roll out small quantities of dough, working quickly so that the dough will not take up too much sugar. Cut in ring shapes. Bake for 12 minutes or until golden brown.

Yields 6 dozen.

SOFT MOLASSES COOKIES

1 cup sugar
1 cup melted bacon fat
1 cup molasses
2 tablespoons vinegar
2 tablespoons cold water
2 teaspoons baking soda
quarter teaspoon each of ginger, cloves, cinnamon
4 cups flour
Mix all well together, roll out to 1/4" thick. Bake at 275° for eight to ten minutes.

From Virginia Leavitt (Mrs. John F.), 1988

VIRGINIA LEAVITT got this recipe from her husband John's mother Grace, who was born in Norway, Maine, but who lived on the coast near Thomaston where John grew up. It is typical of most Maine soft molasses cookies, even down to the vinegar. These cookies would work nicely and give the calories a fisherman or sailor needed aboard vessels where drippings were easier to come by than butter.

Mrs. Leavitt's ingredient list is sufficient, but I will elaborate on the process. You may wish to substitute melted vegetable shortening, lard, or margarine for the bacon fat. Ovens vary, and you may find that 300° for ten minutes gives you better results; take a taste from your first pan full to decide.

Preheat oven to 275°. Grease a couple of cookie sheets. Sift together dry ingredients. Mix together the sugar, melted bacon fat, and molasses. Then add the vinegar and cold water. Stir in dry ingredients. Roll out on a floured board to a quarter of an inch thick, cut in rounds, and place on a greased cookie sheet. Bake for 8-10 minutes. Put on rack to cool.

Yields 5 dozen 2-inch cookies.

SADIES COOKIES

2 cups sugar
1 cup butter
2 eggs. One tablespoon of wine
1 Teaspoons soda in 1/4 cups milk
Flour to roll.

From *Wharves, Piers, and Slips,* 1867, collection of G.W. Blunt White Library

THIS HANDWRITTEN RECIPE is one of twenty-two written on the blank pages of a report prepared for commissioners in charge of the port of New York wharves, piers, and slips. We do not know who the person was who wrote them but here is a nice, perfectly useful sugar cookie typically for the nineteenth century, a bit imprecise by modern standards.

These turn out buttery, sweet, and crisp. You can vary them by adding more or less flour. With more flour they are less buttery and crisp but are easier to handle. You can also vary them by rolling them thickly or thinly. With the amount of flour specified, you will get a tender dough, and the cookie will spread when you bake it.

These cookies make a very good snickerdoodle-style cookie, roll small balls between your hands, roll in cinnamon sugar and place them on the cookie sheet to spread into nice round cookies. If you prefer use vanilla or lemon extract, instead of wine, for flavoring.

1 teaspoon baking soda
3 cups of flour
2 cups sugar
1 cup butter
2 eggs, beaten slightly
1 tablespoon wine (Marsala, tawny port, cream sherry)
1/4 cup milk

Preheat oven to 375°. Grease a couple of cookie sheets. Sift together the flour and baking soda. Cream together the sugar and butter. Beat in the eggs and wine; beat well then add milk. Add the dry ingredients to make a tender dough. Chill the dough for at least an hour. On a lightly floured board, roll out about a quarter of the dough to about a quarter of an inch thick, cut and place on a cookie sheet about an inch and a half apart. Alternatively, roll teaspoon-sized pieces between your floured hands, and place about 2 inches apart on the cookie sheet.

Bake about nine to ten minutes, or until golden brown. Allow to cool and harden slightly on the cookie sheet before removing them to cooling racks.

Yields 8-10 dozen, 2" to 3" cookies.

LAFAYETTE GINGERBREAD

Five eggs
Half a pound of brown sugar
Half a pound of fresh butter
a pint of shugar [sic] house molasses
A pound and half of flour
Four tablespoons of ginger
Two large stiks [sic] of cinnamon Powdered
Three dozen grain of allspice and sifted
Three dozen of cloves
The juice and grated peel of two large lemons
A little pearlash or salratus [sic]
Stir the butter to a cream
Beat the eggs very well

Pour the molasses at once into the butter and sugar add the ginger and other spice and stir all well together

Put in the eggs and flour alternately stirring all the time stir the whole very hard and put the lemon in at last when the whole is mixed stir it till very light. Butter an earthen pan or a thick tin or iron one and put the gingerbread in it.

Bake it in a moderate oven an hour or more according to its thickness take care that it does not burn Or you may bake it in small cakes or little tins it lightness will be much improved by a small teaspoonful of vinegar and stirred lightly in at the last too much pearlash will give it an unpleasant taste If you use pearlash you must omit the lemon as its tast [sic] will be entirely destroyed by the pearlash you substitute for the lemon some raisins and currants well floured to prevent their sinking

From *Elam Eldredge Papers*, 1830-1851, collection of G.W. Blunt White Library

THOMAS ELDREDGE of Mystic copied this recipe from Eliza Leslie's *Seventy Five Receipts* published in Philadelphia in 1828. Named in all likelihood for the French general the Marquis de Lafayette, who had assisted the colonies in their war of independence, and who had revisited the young republic on a triumphal tour in 1824, this gingerbread is nicely spicy and when made with lemon is very good and a bit unusual. The original recipe makes a large quantity but in the following instructions I have halved it. The terms saleratus and pearlash refer to early chemical leavens and I have substituted baking soda for them.

2-3/4 cups flour
2 teaspoons baking soda
2 tablespoons of ginger
2 teaspoons cinnamon
3/4 teaspoon allspice
3/4 teaspoon cloves
1/2 cup butter
1/3 cup light brown sugar,
  tightly packed
1 cup of molasses
3 large eggs, beaten
Juice and grated peel of one large lemon

Preheat the oven to 350°. Grease and flour a 9" x 9" pan. Sift the dry ingredients together and set aside. Cream the butter and add the sugar and molasses, beating well. Add the eggs and lemon juice. Beat in the dry ingredients until you have a smooth batter. Pour into the baking pan, and bake for 50 to 60 minutes. It is done when top springs back to the touch or when tester inserted comes out clean.

9 Pie and Pastry

FOR MOST OF THE 1800 NEW ENGLANDERS favored pie over most other sweets for a dessert. Almost any fruit in any season was suitable for pie, and early cookbook recipes merely suggest which spice to choose without specifying much else. Manuscript recipe collections seldom include pie fillings since the process was so familiar, common, and easy. Pie-making was another of the steward's chores aboard ship, so that the captain and first officers might enjoy a slab after dinner.

Pies are nearly immune to failure in a fireplace oven, since they will not fall if you should jostle them in the oven, and will continue baking when you close the oven up after checking it. They are also very easy to bake in a bake kettle down-hearth, it is the perfect dessert for a hearth cooked meal.

If you plan to bake your pies in a fireplace oven, you will want to have them assembled and ready to go as soon as the oven is raked out. The high initial temperature is good, and the gradual drop finishes them nicely. Put them to one side of the oven and the bread if you are baking together you can remove one without disturbing the other.

Large Cheese PUMPKIN. A splendid variety for pies, and all family use. Fine grain, sweet and solid. Very productive. ℔.60, ½℔.35, ¼℔.20, oz.7, pkt.4,

PASTRY

Take a quantity of flour proportioned to the number of pies you wish to make, then rub in some lard and salt, and stir it up with cold water; then roll it out, and spread on some lard, and scatter over some dry flour; then double it together, and cut it in pieces, and roll it to the thickness you wish to use it.

From *New England Economical Housekeeper*, by Mrs. E.A. Howland, 1845

MRS. HOWLAND'S RECIPE for pastry seems vague to us but would not have been for the experienced nineteenth-century cook. Lard was a common shortening, as was butter, and puff pastry was another popular choice.

A good rule of thumb when making crust is, if you don't measure for flour and shortening, is to squeeze a handful of the mixture which should cling together; then add enough cold water until it all sticks when mixed. My own favorite pie-crust recipe follows.

PIE CRUST

2 cups of flour (half whole wheat pastry flour and half white, if you wish)
1 teaspoon salt
2/3 cup shortening
6-8 tablespoons ice water

Mix together the flour(s) and salt. Cut the shortening into the flour with a pastry blender or rub it in with your fingers. Add the ice water one tablespoon at a time, tossing the mixture with a rubber spatula or a spoon until it all will stick together. Put in the refrigerator to chill.

When you are ready to make a pie, divide the crust into two parts, and, handling it as little as possible, roll out quickly to size; fold in half, and in half again, place point in center of the pie dish and unfold.

Add the filling, and if the pie requires a top crust repeat the process above, crimping the edges to close them.

Yields two 9-inch pie crusts.

DRIED APPLE PIE

Stew the apples soft, turn them into a pan and mash them fine. Add half the peel of a lemon cut fine, or a little grated nutmeg, a sprinkle of salt, molasses or sugar to make them quite sweet. Bake them in a rich paste a little over half an hour. This will be quite as good as fresh fruit.

From *The Complete Domestic Guide,* by Mrs. L.G. Abell, 1853

YOU MIGHT THINK THAT STEWED and mashed dried apples cooked even more in a pie shell. They aren't. And another nice thing about them is that they do not collapse as fresh apples do, leaving the top crust high and dry.

Because the apples are already cooked, the main object in baking is to get the crust done. If you wish, use the pastry recipe on page 172, rolling it out as the old recipe suggests with additional shortening to create a rich crust. This recipe makes a lemony flavored pie; if you prefer it less lemony, reduce the amount of peel, or just use a table-spoon of juice. A more specific interpretation follows.

3/4 to one pound of dried apples
Water
Grated peel of 1/2 lemon
1/2 teaspoon nutmeg
1/4 cup molasses or
  1/2 cup brown sugar
Salt
Pastry enough for two 9-inch crusts

Preheat oven to 400°

Put the dried apples into a pan and add water until you just see it through the apples. Stew gently till the apples are quite soft. Then mash with the back of a spoon. Add the lemon peel, nutmeg, molasses or sugar, and a dash of salt, to the mashed apples and mix. Taste and adjust seasoning if you wish.

Line a pie plate with one crust, and fill it with the apple mixture, top with another crust. Bake at 400° for 10 minutes, then reduce oven to 375° and bake an additional 20 minutes, or until the crust is done.

Yields one 9-inch pie.

APPLE PIE

When you make apple pies, stew your apples very little indeed; just strike them through, to make them tender. Some people do not stew them at all, but cut them up in very thin slices, and lay them in the crust. Pies made in this way may retain more of the spirit of the apple; but I do not think the seasoning mixes in as well. Put in sugar to your taste; it is impossible to make a precise rule, because apples vary so much in acidity. A very little salt, and a small piece of butter in each pie, makes them richer. Cloves and cinnamon are both suitable spice. Lemon brandy and rose-water are both excellent. A wineglassful of each is sufficient for three or four pies. If your apples lack spirit, grate in a whole lemon.

From *The American Frugal Housewife,* by Mrs. Child, 1833

THIS RECIPE FROM the earlier part of the century sums up just about everything that could be said about apple pies. There is a great tradition of apple-pie eating in this country and there are many references to the frequency of it being served and eaten. Yet not one of the dozen or so manuscript recipe notebooks I own contains an apple pie recipe. Period apple pie recipes are found almost exclusively in printed cookbooks. That makes me believe that it was one of many dishes that was commonly prepared without benefit of a strict recipe. When apple pie recipes do occur in cookbooks, they either have some special little fillip (like adding a few spoonfuls of cream to the filling), or describe the process painstakingly for the uninitiated cook, or they say basically what Mrs. Child did in the recipe above.

There are several things of interest to note in Mrs. Child's recipe. First, she

recommended stewing the apples before putting them in a pie, apparently more usual in the nineteenth century. Today we almost always make them from raw apples, which Mrs. Child acknowledged "some people" did then.

Second, she noted that "apples vary so much in acidity," which was certainly the case in the nineteenth century, when there were more varieties available than today. Apples varied in keeping qualities, ripening times, acidity, value for cooking or cider-making, and, of course, flavor. So the addition of sugar was a subjective decision, not quantifiable for a recipe.

Third, she commented on lemon brandy and rosewater "sufficient for three or four pies," which underlines the nineteenth-century habit of making pies in large batches.

Other recipes, both from Mrs. Child's time and later, recommended lemon juice or peel for apple pie, and added nutmeg to the list of suggested spices. Rosewater is still available today, and you may like to try a bit sometime. Remember that a wine-glassful is about a quarter cup, and if that is sufficient for three or four pies then a tablespoonful should be sufficient for one pie.

If you have not yet had the experience of cooking without a precise, scientific recipe, then making an apple pie under Mrs. Child's tutelage is a good way to start. Just don't worry about it; taste as you go, and remember that if you use raw apples they will shrink, so you will want to pile them high.

APPLE PIE FILLING

6-8 medium apples, peeled (if you wish) and cored
1 tablespoon rosewater or lemon brandy
1/2 cup of light brown sugar
1 tablespoon of flour
1 teaspoon cinnamon (or to taste)
1/2 teaspoon cloves or nutmeg
2 tablespoons of butter, cut into pieces

Preheat the oven to 425°. Slice the apples into a large bowl. Add rosewater or brandy first, and toss until the apples are coated then add the sugar, flour, and spices. Toss until the apples are evenly coated. Empty into the pie plate lined with your preferred pie crust, and dot the top with pieces of butter. Lay a top crust on and crimp the edges. Slash the top crust in a few places. Bake for ten minutes at 425° then reduce the temperature to 350° and bake for another 45 to 50 minutes. Look for bubbling and/or test the apples with a sharp knife to see if they are soft. Remove and eat warm with a slice of cheddar cheese tucked just under the crust.

MINCEMEAT PIES

...Small pieces of butter sliced over the mince before laying on the top crust, will make them keep longer...

From *New England Economical Housekeeper,* by Mrs. E.A. Howland, 1845

WEIGHT- AND cholesterol-conscious modern people will probably be reluctant to add butter to suet-laden mincemeat. Mrs. Child says bits of sweet butter "makes them [the pies] rich; but these are not necessary." Most of us will agree. Two to two-and-a-half cups of mincemeat per 9-inch pie is the usual amount of filling these days, but I think that makes a skimpy pie so I use up to a quart per pie, topped with a lattice crust. Bake at 350° for 45 minutes. For mincemeat, see Preserves, Chapter 10, page 184.

PUMPKIN PIE

Pare the pumkins [sic], cut them into small pieces, and stew them in just enough water to prevent their burning; let them stand over a slow fire until they are quite soft, then strain them through a collander [sic], and to one quart of pumkin, add one quart of rich milk, one table-spoonful of ginger, one tea-spoonful of salt, one nutmeg, two tea-cups of sugar—more will be necessary if you use brown sugar— and four eggs, well beaten; when cold, put into deep plates, lined with Paste, No. 1, trim and bake forty-five minutes.

From *The Practical Cookbook*, by Mrs. Bliss, 1864

THIS HISTORIC RECIPE is obviously for more than one pie. Most modern recipes for a nine-inch pie call for two cups of cooked pumpkin, or half a quart, so the recipe above should yield two pies.

The secret to good pumpkin pies is how well the pumpkin is prepared. Mrs. Abell said to let the cooked pumpkin "remain over the fire, stirring it often until quite dry." If you make this pie from scratch, cooking the pumpkin yourself, is good advice. No liquid should gather in the pumpkin pulp if you have either cooked the pumpkin or drained it long enough in a sieve. Some people now bake the pumpkin instead of boiling or steaming it, and this, too, helps eliminate excess moisture in the pumpkin.

Usually, the sweet little pie pumpkins available in the fall in fruit and vegetable markets are good for one pie. For "rich milk" use whole milk or part whole and half-and-half. One nutmeg grated is equal to three teaspoons, and a tea-cup is equivalent to about half a cup.

2 cups of well-drained cooked pumpkin
1-3/4 cups milk
2 eggs beaten
1 tablespoon of ginger
1/2 teaspoon salt
1 teaspoon freshly grated nutmeg
1 cup of sugar

Preheat oven to 400°. Mix all together very well until the filling is thick and creamy looking. Line your pie plate with pastry, crimping the edges. Pour the pumpkin into it, and bake for 10 minutes at 400° then reduce oven temperature to 350° and bake an additional 30 minutes or until the filling is puffed slightly and firm in the center.

FRUIT AND BERRY PIES

In England, only an upper crust is made. In this country there is generally only an under crust, with bars of paste crossed over the top. I prefer this mode; but these tarts should always be served fresh, or the under crust will become soaked and unwholesome. The berries or fruits are first stewed with sugar to taste, then baked, or not baked in the crust, as preferred.

From *Practical Cooking and Dinner Giving*, by Mrs. Mary F. Henderson, 1882

MRS. HENDERSON IN *Practical Cooking* provided a pastry recipe as well. "For Pies," she said "I mean Yankee pies," distinguishing the favorite American dessert from English tarts. I once heard a story that illustrates the New England attitude toward pie.

An elderly New Englander known for her pies was interviewed by a cookbook writer who asked her what kinds of pies she made.

"Why," she said, "all three kinds."

Amused and a bit condescending, the writer asked her "What three kinds is that?"

"Open, shut, and barred," she answered.

The moral of the story was that New Englanders thought, and still do, that just about anything can be put in a pie. The conventions were and are "open" pies for custard-types, like pumpkin or lemon meringue, "shut" for solid fruited pie such as apple and peach, and "barred" for berry or mince pies, although, of course, there were always variations from these according to personal preferences.

CHERRY PIE

fill with a mix of sour and sweet cherries; sweeten plentifully....Eat fresh....but not warm, with white sugar sifted over the top.

BLACKBERRY PIE

fill with ripe berries, sweetening plentifully....Eat cold with white sugar sifted over.

From *The Dinner Year Book*, by Marion Harland, 1878

ONCE NINETEENTH-CENTURY cooks decided anything could be made into a pie, then pie-filling choices depended on the season or the contents of the preserve cupboards. Interestingly enough, cookbooks included a wide range of berry and fruit pies, but usually left out strawberries, which were favored for eating fresh in other desserts or making preserves. The "recipes" for fruit and berry pies are usually little more than suggestions for the kind of spice and comments on the amount of sweetening—"plentifully," "enough," "less," or "more" than some other sort of fruit. Today we like pie filling thickened, but the period recipes seldom specified a thickening: once in a while a recipe will say "strew some flour over" the fruit in question. Frequently the filling was cooked before being put into the pie.

My favorite modern recipe for blueberry pie follows. It can be used as a filling for a crisp, too, topped with your preferred streusel. I adapt this recipe for use with strawberries, blackberries, and rhubarb.

1 quart of blueberries (generous 4 cups)
Juice of half a lemon
   (about 1-1/2 tablespoons)
Grated rind of lemon (optional)
1/4 cup sugar
1/4 cup light brown sugar
1/4 cup of flour

Preheat the oven to 425°. Line a pie plate with pastry. Toss all ingredients together in large bowl and then fill the plate. Top with a lattice crust. Bake at 425° for 10 minutes, then reduce the heat to 375° and bake until the filling bubbles, about 35 minutes.

FROSTED LEMON PIES

4 Eggs (Yolks)
2 Lemons
2 Spoons Flour
2 " Melted Butter
9 " White Sugar
1 Cup Milk
Whites of eggs and 3 spoons Sugar for frosting

From the manuscript recipe notebook of Fannie Card, Westerly, Rhode Island, 1879

AS YOU CAN SEE, this is really a recipe for what is now called lemon meringue pie: a lemon-custard filling with a "frosting" of meringue. Lemon pies seem to have come into fashion in the last half of the nineteenth century. The following recipe makes a delicious tangy pie, with a deep meringue.

FILLING

2 lemons, zest and juice
4 tablespoons flour
1 cup milk
4 egg yolks
1 cup sugar
2 tablespoon butter, melted

Prepare a baked pie shell. Grate lemon zest, squeeze juice, mix together and set aside. Whisk a quarter of a cup of milk into the flour, set aside, then put the rest of the milk on to heat up in a double boiler or in a very heavy saucepan. Bring milk just to the boiling point, then whisk in the flour and milk mixture, stirring constantly to avoid lumps; continue to cook, stirring until mixture has thickened. Remove from heat.

Beat together the yolks, sugar, butter, lemon juice and zest, and add that to the milk and flour mixture, returning it to the heat. Cook, stirring, for about 10 minutes or until mixture has the consistency of thick custard and sheets off a spoon. Remove from heat, allow to cool slightly while you prepare the meringue. Then pour the custard into the pie shell.

MERINGUE

Whites of 4 eggs
Pinch of cream of tartar
3 tablespoons sugar

Preheat oven to 350°. Make meringue "frosting" by beating whites till frothy, adding a pinch of cream of tartar, and gradually adding sugar and beating until it makes firm peaks. Spread over the cooled custard, making sure that meringue connects with crust. Set in oven for about 8-10 minutes to brown slightly. Allow to cool entirely so that the filling will set up.

Yields one 8 to 9-inch pie.

BANBURY TARTS

Bann Berries

One cup of sugar, 1 cup seeded raisins chopped, 1 egg, juice of 1 lemon. Put all in a double boiler and cook two minutes.

Make pastry of 2 cups of flour, 1/2 cup lard, 1/2 teaspoon baking powder, a little salt. Roll out and cut thin. Put a teaspoon of raisin mixture in each puff, and bake.

Miss E. Agnes Stewart. From *The Stonington Cookbook*, Reprint of the *Cookbook of the Young People's Society of Christian Endeavor of the Second Congregational Church* (Stonington, Connecticut), ca. 1900

BANBURY TARTS originated in Banbury, Oxfordshire, England, a town known for the number and zeal of its Puritan inhabitants, according to the *Oxford English Dictionary*. The early Banbury cakes were "a small oval cake, of rich pastry with a filling of mincemeat." The filling recipe above has a taste reminiscent of mincemeat.

These are really delicious and easily made from ingredients on hand in nearly anyone's kitchen. The recipe above is clear enough to follow, so an interpretation is not necessary, but I suggest the following procedure: Double the pastry recipe given above because the filling recipe makes enough for up to 40 tarts, use your favorite pastry recipe.

Make the pastry dough and chill it while you are making the filling. You may substitute butter or vegetable shortening for lard in the pastry. You will need 6-8 tablespoons of cold water for the pastry, even though it is not mentioned in the original recipe. Chop the raisins coarsely on a cutting board by rocking a knife through them. Mix the filling ingredients well before cooking. You may also add the grated rind of the lemon for a more lemon-flavored filling. Cook the filling, stirring constantly, until it is slightly thickened. Let it cool completely.

Preheat oven to 425°. Cut the pastry in rounds providing two for each tart. Put the filling on the bottom round, and moisten the edges; then place the top round over, pressing the edges together with a fork. Bake for 15-20 minutes or until golden brown.

Yields up to 40 tarts made with a three-inch cutter.

10 Preserves and Pickles

EARLY AMERICANS WERE SKILLED at many forms of food preservation from careful storage, to dairying, pickling, fermenting, preserving with sugar, salting, drying, smoking, and judicious seasonal management of the food supply to take advantage of cold weather. In the course of the nineteenth century domestic and industrial canning and artificial refrigeration and freezing were added to the repertoire, in some cases replacing some of the other preservation methods. Shipboard diaries and narratives record preservation activities at sea, too, from meat and fish salting to canning fruits and making preserves.

Modern people eat preserved food because it affords variety and not because it is the only way to keep it. Among the recipes below are some tasty possibilities to add variety to your meals. While some of the recipes were performed in fireplaces, you will probably prefer to use them in your modern kitchen so fireplace instructions will not be provided. Acquaint yourself with modern sanitation rules with preserves and bear in mind as you use the old recipes.

EXTRA EARLY EGYPTIAN BEET.

A very dark red, and fine sort for family use. One of the earliest and best varieties for gardeners use in bunching for market. Is smooth and so very early, that good high prices can always be secured. The quality is excellent, and a supply kept continuously, by repeated sowings. ℔. 40, ½ ℔. 25, ¼ ℔. 15, oz. 6, pkt. 4.

MINCEMEAT

Boil a tender, nice piece of beef—any piece that is clear of sinews and gristle; boil it till it is perfectly tender. When it is cold, chop it very fine, and be very careful to get out every particle of bone and gristle. The suet is sweeter and better to boil half an hour or more in the liquor the beef has been boiled in; but few people do this. Pare, core, and chop the apples fine. If you use raisins, stone them. If you use currants, wash and dry them at the fire. Two pounds of beef after it is chopped; three quarters of a pound of suet; one pound and a quarter of sugar; three pounds of apples; two pounds of currants, or raisins. Put in a gill of brandy; lemon brandy is better, if you have any prepared. Make it quite moist with new cider. I should not think a quart would be too much;... A very little pepper...One ounce of cinnamon, one ounce of cloves. Two nutmegs add to the pleasantness of the flavor;...If your apples are rather sweet, grate in a whole lemon.

From *The American Frugal Housewife*, by Mrs. Child, 1833

WE DON'T THINK OF mincemeat as a preserve, but in fact, in early times it was a way to preserve fresh meat, including sometimes beef tongue or venison, for future use. It was very often made in the fall when apples were plentiful. Old mincemeat recipes vary to include lemons and oranges, both juice and rind, citron, and wine, in addition to the standard meat, apples, suet, raisins, currants, and spices. You can refrigerate it, process it in canning jars, or store it in a crock in a cold place.

This recipe makes a really delicious and hearty mincemeat. Modern mincemeat has no meat, or scarcely any, and is gluey with cornstarch rather than unctuous with suet. Allow the mincemeat to season for a week or two before you use it in a pie; the flavor will develop and mellow.

2 lbs. lean beef
3/4 lb. beef suet

3 lbs. apples
2 lbs. currants or raisins or 1 lb. of each
3 cups brown sugar, firmly packed
1/2 cup brandy
1 quart sweet cider
1 teaspoon pepper
2 teaspoons salt
2-1/2 tablespoons cinnamon
2-1/2 tablespoons cloves
2 tablespoons nutmeg

Boil the beef till fork-tender. Cook the beef suet for a half hour in the beef liquor. Allow both to drain and cool enough to be firm. Chop finely by hand in a wooden bowl, by running through a grinder, or pulsing it in a food processor. Peel, core, and chop apples finely. Chop the currants and raisins. Mix all the meat, suet, and fruit together. Add the brandy, cider, and spices. Mix all together. Pack into a crock and store in a cool place, or pack into canning jars and process to seal.

Yields 4 quarts.

PICKLED CABBAGE

Cabbage, White, Pickled.

Slice your cabbage thin; then lay it in salt for twenty-four hours, strain it very dry, then put it in a stone jar with allspice, mace, and vinegar, and pour it on boiling hot; tie it very close, repeat the vinegar three times, and it will be fit for use.

From *Practical American Cookery and Domestic Economy,* by Miss Hall, 1855

RED CABBAGE SEEMS to have been slightly more popular for pickling than green or, as Miss Hall described it, white. But the instructions for white and red pickled cabbage are similar and seem to have no counterpart in modern cookbooks. Do not confuse pickled cabbage with sauerkraut, which is a fermented product created by salting cabbage and letting nature have her way. Sauerkraut was not typically a New England dish and does not commonly appear in manuscript sources or imprints.

Miss Hall was very modest in her choice of spices; in other sources, ginger, cloves, and black peppercorns were also listed as spices suitable for pickled cabbage. Most recipes recommend pouring on hot vinegar, repeating that operation on subsequent days till the cabbage is tender. Most agree that salting for at least a day improves the pickle. Mrs. Child said to let the cabbage remain in pickle "eight to ten days before you eat them."

Modern distilled vinegar is probably sharper than it was in the nineteenth century; you can approximate the earlier type by adding water to your vinegar until it is still sharp but palatable. Although most modern instructions for pickling emphasize the need for sufficient acidity to preserve vegetables safely, keep in mind that Miss Hall did not intend anyone to keep this cabbage for a long time. You may want to store the pickled cabbage in the refrigerator if you don't intend to eat it right away. Serve this in small portions or as a salad.

1 pound cabbage or 4-6 cups shredded
1/2 cup pickling salt
1 cup vinegar mixed into 3 cups water
1 teaspoon each your choice of:
    whole allspice, blade mace, cloves,
    black peppercorns, and whole dried
    ginger root

Shred cabbage, and toss it with the pickling salt. Let it stand overnight. Next day, drain it and turn onto a towel to soak up excess moisture.

Heat the vinegar, water, and spices in a non-reactive saucepan. When boiling hot, remove from fire. Put the shredded cabbage into large sterilized glass jars and pour the hot vinegar over it, dividing the spices among the jars. Close the jar tightly. In two or three days, open the jar, drain off the vinegar, reheat and put back over the cabbage.

In another two or three days, repeat this. At the end of the next two days, taste the cabbage and, if you wish, repeat heating the vinegar again.

Store the finished cabbage in the refrigerator or, if you wish, process and seal it in canning jars according to the usual canning procedure for pickles.

Yields about 3 cups pickled cabbage.

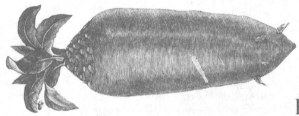

PICKLED BEETS

BEETS. Break off the leaves, but do not cut beets, as that spoils both flavor and appearance; wash them and boil them till tender; then take them out into basin of cold water, and rub all the outside skin off, with the hands; then slice them thin in a dish, and just cover them with cold vinegar, and sprinkle them with pepper and salt, or quarter them, and lay them for a day or two in cold vinegar, as they are then fit for use. The tips of young beets are dressed as asparagus.

From *Practical American Cookery and Domestic Economy,* by Miss Hall, 1855

BEETS WOULD TRAVEL WELL on a ship. Pickling them would have been a good way to use leftover boiled beets. Mary Lawrence on the whale ship *Addison* reported having pickled beets for Christmas dinner but didn't say how they were prepared, although one period cookbook recommended spiced vinegar.

This recipe is clear enough that an adaptation is not needed. You may find today's vinegar a bit too sharp, and you may wish to dilute it to taste with water. If you decide to use spices, a bit of whole allspice, ginger, mace, and mustard seed would be appropriate, or even pre-packaged pickling spice.

BRANDIED PEACHES

The Temperance movement in the early nineteenth century inhibited some preserving with brandy but some cooks made a distinction between drinking brandy and using it to cook or preserve with. After all one would become heartily sick of eating brandied peaches before one felt tipsy.

Most early instructions for brandied peaches called for the old fashioned pound-for-pound formula of one pound of sugar for every pound of fruit, adding brandy to the resulting syrup. To approximate early brandied peaches, you would do well to find a good workable canned peaches recipe, using a heavy syrup—heating together equal quantities of water and sugar—to pour over the skinned peaches, to which you add your preferred amount of brandy, up to a 1/2 cup of brandy to each pint of canned peaches. Seal according to instructions for canned peaches, and let them stand a week to develop flavor.

Or follow the slightly different instructions below.

8 quarts of peaches
Sugar
1 quart of brandy

Scald the peaches and skin them by rubbing the skin off gently. Weigh them and measure out an equal quantity of sugar. Put the peaches into an earthenware crock or over-sized glass jar. Sprinkle the sugar over each layer of peaches as you add them to the container. When you have done this with all the peaches, add the brandy to the container. Cover with a clean cloth and set in a cool place for at least two months. Check from time to time to make sure they do not form mold on the top. If it should form, merely skim it off and recover. Taste them and when they are ready, can them according to the usual instructions for canned peaches.

Makes 6-8 quarts.

PICKLED PEACHES

Take those of full growth, ripe, but not soft; wipe them with a flannel cloth, or pare them; stick three or four cloves into each peach; lay them in a stone jar. Put half a pound of sugar to a quart of good vinegar, add cinnamon and other spices to the taste; let the vinegar come to a boil, skim, and pour it on the peaches. Let them stand two weeks, then pour off the vinegar and boil it, and pour it on again, and they are then fit for use.

From *Practical American Cookery and Domestic Economy,* by Miss Hall, 1855

IN THE EARLY nineteenth century, pickled peaches were more pickles than peaches. As the century wore on, this dish became sweeter. By the turn of the century it was even named "sweet pickled peaches," and had the generous modern ratio of two parts of sugar to every part of vinegar, instead of the one to four parts suggested by Hall. Pears were routinely treated like peaches in pickling.

You could try this recipe as it stands, canning the peaches instead of keeping them in a stoneware jar. Brown sugar is often mentioned by later cookbooks for pickled peaches, so you may wish to use that instead of white sugar. Or you may prefer to use the modernized recipe.

8 pounds of peaches
3-4 whole cloves per peach
2 cups cider vinegar
3-1/2 cups of white sugar
2 sticks of cinnamon

Scald the peaches by pouring boiling water over them, and then rub the skins off. Stick cloves into each peach. Dissolve the sugar in the vinegar and boil them together with the cinnamon for about five minutes, then add the peaches until they are heated through. Put the peaches into sterilized pint jars and top off the jars with the vinegar and sugar syrup, allowing half an inch head room. Seal and process for 10 minutes in a boiling water bath.

Yields about four pints.

PRESERVED ORANGE PEEL

Weigh the oranges whole, and allow pound to pound; peel the oranges neatly, and cut the rinds into narrow shreds; boil until tender, changing the water twice, replenishing with hot from the tea-kettle; squeeze the strained juice of the oranges over sugar; heat this to a boil. Put in the shreds, and boil twenty minutes. Lemon-peel can be preserved in the same way, only allowing more sugar.

From *The Hearthstone; or Life at Home, A Household Manual,* by Laura C. Halloway, 1887

PRESERVED PEEL OF either lemon or orange is a frequent ingredient for nineteenth century steamed puddings and mincemeat. The recipe above calls for sugar in an equal proportion to the weight of the oranges (pound to pound). An average orange weighs approximately six ounces, so 3/4 of a cup is a good proportion to each orange.

I prefer a thinner-skinned juice orange to the thick-skinned navel oranges for this project. Navel oranges have brittle skin. Cutting the peel into the julienne strips needed is easier to do if you use a sharp pair of kitchen scissors.

This recipe makes the most delicious candied orange peel I have ever tasted. If you want sugared peel, roll the shreds of orange in granulated sugar and lay them on waxed paper to dry before putting them away in a jar.

Thin-skinned oranges
3/4 cup sugar per orange
1-1/2 cups hot water per orange
 (or plenty of water to cover the peels)

Cut the oranges in half; squeeze out juice and reserve it. Scrape away the white part of the peel and cut the skin into julienne strips; using scissors makes it easy. Put the shreds into the hot water and boil for about five minutes; drain; pour on more hot water; boil another five minutes; drain; boil a third time for five minutes, and drain.

Strain the juice and add to the sugar in a heavy saucepan, bring to a boil, then add the cooked orange peel. Boil gently for 20 minutes.

Remove with slotted spoon and cool on waxed paper, separating the pieces of peel and rolling them, if you wish, in sugar.

Yields about an ounce of candied peel per orange, but this will vary depending on your oranges.

QUINCE PRESERVES

Preserved Quinces

Pare and core your quinces, take the cores and skins and boil them an hour, then strain the juice all out through a coarse cloth; boil your quinces in this juice till they are tender, then take them out; add the weight of the quinces in clean sugar to the sirup, boil it and skim it till it is clean; then put in your quinces again, and boil them three hours, when they are done. Preserves should not be covered up till entirely cold. They should be set away in stone jars.

From *New England Economical Housekeeper*, by Mrs. E.A. Howland, 1845

PINEAPPLE PRESERVES

Pine Apples.

Take those that are ripe and fresh; pare off the rind, and cut in slices about half an inch thick. Sprinkle between them powdered loaf sugar, and let them remain until the next day. Then with the usual syrup boil until tender, putting them in when it is cold. Keep in a cool place.

From *Practical American Cookery and Domestic Economy*, by Miss Hall, 1855

Preserved Pineapples

Pare the pineapple, and carefully remove the eyes with a sharp pointed knife. Either chop or grate the pineapple, or shred it with a fork, rejecting the core. Weigh, and allow three-quarters of a pound of sugar to each pound of fruit. Put all together in the preserving kettle, stir well, stand aside overnight. In the morning, bring to a boil, skim and cook slowly. Pour it into jars, and seal.

From *Ayer's Preserve Book*, ca. 1895

MISS HALL AND OTHERS cautioned cooks that potential difficulties with making preserves were that they could ferment, get moldy, or become candied. On a ship at sea, fermentation and mold would be the two most likely storage problems. Candying was caused by processing the fruit too long at too high a temperature.

When Mrs. Lawrence put up her "famous lot of pineapples," on the whale ship *Addison*, we have no way of knowing whether she intended long- or short-term storage. She may have made a pineapple jam or marmalade that she could have brought home to New Bedford, or perhaps she prepared the pineapples as canned fruit. Both of these methods were regarded as "preserving."

The first recipe above was satisfactory as a method of short-term preserving. Its inclusion in Miss Hall's book gave cooks ashore a way of stretching a treat of pineapples a little longer.

The "usual syrup" could be whatever you prefer: a light syrup of half as much sugar as water, a medium of three quarter as much sugar as water, or a heavy syrup of equal proportions of sugar and water. Be sure to use the liquid that collects after the pineapples have stood with their light sprinkling of sugar. If you use this recipe literally, keep the pineapples in the fridge. Or you can process by cooking them in the syrup for about five minutes, packing them hot in sterilized jars, allowing half an inch headroom,

and processing in a boiling-water bath for 20 minutes.

The second recipe yields a jam-like pineapple preserve and comes from a later recipe book from Mrs. Lawrence's time. But the relative scarcity of pineapples for preserving until later in the century may account for the scarcity of pineapple-preserve recipes in the middle of the nineteenth century. The low-pectin pineapple does not set up as readily as other fruits so this jam is very tender. It is most suitable as a sauce or cake filling. Modern cooks may wish to take advantage of liquid pectin in the following adapted recipe.

1 pineapple (about 4 lbs.)
Sugar
3 oz. liquid pectin

Pare and core the pineapple, and shred into a bowl to catch the juice. Measure the pineapple pulp and juice. Measure out three quarters as much sugar (about 2 cups) as pulp and juice, and mix together in a preserving kettle. Let stand overnight.

Next day, bring the pineapple and sugar mixture to a hard boil, and boil for a minute. Remove it from the heat and stir in the pectin, and bring to a boil again for a minute. Remove from the fire once again and continue stirring for another five minutes to keep the bits of fruit suspended. Pour into jars and seal.

Yields about four half-pint jars.

MARMALADES

They may be made of any fruits without seeds. The fruit should be boiled very soft with some of the kernals; and all of the pits of quinces, and parings, boiled and strained, added to the sugar. Mash to a fine pulp, and add sugar in the proportions of the sweetmeat, and simmer thick. It should be a smooth thick mass. Put up in tumblers.

From *The Complete Domestic Guide*, by Mrs. L.G. Abell, 1853

PRESERVED QUINCES could be served as a dish for tea or made into marmalade. On board the whale ship *Tiger*, the captain's wife Mary Brewster may have used a supply of fresh quinces for either once the supply of fresh fruit was gone.

"Pound for pound" was the rule of thumb for most nineteenth-century preserving; that is, one pound of sugar for every pound of fruit, or, as Mrs. Howland said, "the weight of the quinces in sugar." While Howland suggested putting the quinces away in stone jars, you may wish to can yours. Use a hot pack and process for 20 minutes in a boiling-water bath.

The second recipe is a good general instruction for that sort of preserve—as the recipe notes, for fruits that "do not have seeds" (as strawberries or raspberries have). Seeded fruits were usually made into jam. Again this is a pound for pound type of preserve. Quinces are high in pectin so you should have no trouble getting the marmalade to jell, which you can test by seeing if a spoonful sets up in cold water.

CANNED WHORTLEBERRIES

Preserved Whortleberries

#244. To preserve Whortleberries, for Winter Use.

Put the berries in a bottle, then cork and seal it, place the bottle in a kettle of cold water, and gradually let it boil. As soon as it boils, take it off and let it cool; then take the bottles out and put them away for winter use.

Gooseberries, plums, and currants, may be preserved in the same manner.

From *New England Economical Housekeeper*, by Mrs. E.A. Howland, 1845

TO PRESERVE FRUITS FOR TARTS OR OTHER FAMILY DESSERTS

Cherries, plums of all sorts, and apples, gather when ripe, and lay them in small jars that will hold a pound; strew over each jar six ounces of good loaf sugar, pounded; cover with two bladders, each separately tied down; then put the jars up to the neck in a large stewpan of water, and let it boil gently for three hours. All sorts of fruits should be kept free from damp.

From *Practical American Cookery and Domestic Economy,* by Miss Hall, 1855

CANNING

This is a most valuable manner of preserving vegetables and fruit....I also advise the canning of sweetmeats of every kind. In that case the same amount of sugar is not required, and the fruit does not have to be boiled until the natural flavor is entirely lost. If glass jars are used instead of cans, they must be put on the fire in cold water with a plate or piece of wood in the bottom of the kettle. They should not be filled until the water is boiling, and when they are cold the covers should be tightened, as the glass will contract a little after cooling.

From *Practical Cooking and Dinner Giving,* by Mrs. Mary F. Henderson, 1882

THESE three sets of instructions are included for your interest, and to demonstrate that Fred and Sallie Smith of the whaling bark *Ohio* in 1877 would have been familiar with canning procedures for fruits like whortleberries for pot pie. Imagine what a chore this would have been on board ship.

LEMON BRANDY

Have a bottle full of brandy with as large a mouth as any bottle you have, into which you cut your lemon and orange peel when they are fresh and sweet. This brandy gives a delicious flavor to all sots of pies, puddings, and cakes. Lemon is the pleasantest spice of the two; therefore they should be kept in separate bottles.

From *American Frugal Housewife*, by L. Maria Child, 1833

THIS IS A VERY EASY way to add authentic lemon flavoring to nineteenth-century dishes. Mrs. Child uses the lemon brandy as we do lemon extract, though slightly more is needed per spoonful. A wide mouth mayonnaise or canning jar is perfect for this. Merely put a pint of brandy into the jar, and add the lemon peels as you squeeze them for their juice. Taste the brandy from time to time, and when you have a satisfactory flavor, remove the peels and use the brandy.

SEA CATCHUP

Take a gallon of stale strong beer, a pound of anchovies washed from the pickle, a pound of peeled shallot or small onions, half an ounce of mace, half an ounce of cloves, a quarter of an ounce of whole pepper, three or four large pieces of ginger, two quarts of large mushrooms—flaps rubbed to pieces. Put the whole into a kettle closely covered, and let it simmer slowly till reduced to one half. Then strain it through a flannel bag, and let it stand till quite cold before you bottle it. Have small bottles and fill them quite full of the catchup. Dip the corks in melted rosin.

This catchup keeps well at sea, and may be taken into any part of the world. A spoonful of it mixed in melted butter will make a fine fish sauce. It may also be used to flavor gravy.

From Eliza Leslie, *Directions for Cookery in Its Various Branches*, 1851

MOST CATCHUP in the eighteenth and nineteenth centuries was not made from tomatoes but instead was more similar to Worcestershire sauce or a Thai fish sauce. Imagine a clove flavored soy sauce with anchovies in it, and that just about sums up this recipe. The word catchup is derived from the Amoy dialect of Chinese *koechiap* or *ketsiap* which is a brine of pickled fish or shellfish, and the Malay word *ketsiap* refers to a fermented fish sauce. Now that Thai and Vietnamese cookery is so popular, fish sauces are not the strangers that they were even 20 years ago. The sauces were introduced to English cookery along with curry and other foods via the spice trades.

Mushrooms and walnuts were also pickled and the liquid was saved to make catsups by those names as well.

SEA CATSUP

2 quarts stale strong beer (preferably a dark beer)
8 ounces anchovies, drained and rinsed in hot water to remove the oil
8 ounces of shallots or onions, coarsely chopped
2 teaspoons mace
1 heaping tablespoon cloves
1 heaping teaspoon whole peppercorns
2-inch pieces of fresh ginger, sliced
4 cups mushrooms coarsely chopped.

Open the beer and empty it into an enamel or stainless steel pot with a tight-fitting lid. Give it a brisk stir and allow it to sit until it is flat. Add all the rest of the ingredients and, with the lid on, bring it to a boil. Remove the lid, reduce the temperature, and let it simmer at a low temperature until the quantity has reduced to one half (about three hours). Strain it through a sieve lined with several layers of cheesecloth. Let it cool. Bottle it. Store in a refrigerator.

Yield about three cups.

11 Sailor's Dishes

THE COLORFUL NAMES SAILORS so often gave their food lead us to think that sea-going dishes were entirely different from anything eaten ashore. Not so. In the recipes that follow, you will recognize that plum duff is scarcely different from steamed puddings in the dessert chapter, that roly-poly pudding is similar to apple dumplings, and lobscouse is a stew. What a deep-water sailor ate depended entirely upon where in the ship's hierarchy he stood. Fresh home-style food—meat, vegetables, and freshly baked bread—was prepared for the captain and first officers. The sailors ate salt beef and pork, hardtack, and had allowances of potatoes, rice, or other vegetables. Dessert in the form of duff came twice a week with molasses for sauce.

Shipboard cooking facilities put an emphasis on boiling and the oven yielded up occasional baked goods mostly for the cabin. By doing favors for the cook, like splitting wood or scrubbing pots, sailors could negotiate the special privilege of using the oven to make a favorite snack, dandyfunk.

PLUM DUFF

1 pound of flour
pinch of salt
1 teaspoon soda
6 oz. raisins
2 teaspoons cream of tartar
4 oz. sugar
2 oz. drippings

Sift the flour, soda, cream of tartar, and salt together and add the drippings. Stone the raisins and add the sugar. Mix all together with water. Make into balls and boil for 4 hours or steam for 5 hours. If allowed, serve with sweet sauce.

From *The Yankee Whaler*, by Clifford Ashley, 1938

CLIFFORD ASHLEY SHIPPED from New Bedford on the whaling bark *Sunbeam* in August of 1904 this plum duff recipe is typical of most simple boiled puddings of the time and is a top-of-the-line pudding for the fo'c'sle. Plain duff was for Sunday and possibly one other weekday, while plum duff was served in the fo'c'sle only on holidays and special occasions. During most of the 1800s ship's cooks probably did not put sugar in fo'c'sle duff. Molasses was almost always served as sauce.

Frederick Harlow, a foremast hand on the *Akbar* in 1875, described a duff made with dried apples instead of raisins, which was one of the common shipboard variations on plum duff.

This duff is delicious. If you boil it in a cloth, expect the exterior to be like the bottom side of a dumpling. The texture is moist and cake-like. You may prefer

to steam it in a pudding bowl or mold. You can always add spices and more raisins. The recipe above makes two duffs, which is enough for two dozen people; the following recipe is half the original. At least once, try eating it with molasses drizzled on it as sailors did.

2 cups flour
1/2 teaspoon baking soda
1 teaspoon cream of tartar
Pinch of salt
1/4 cup melted shortening
1/4 cup sugar
2/3 cup raisins
2/3 cup water

Set a large pot of water on and heat to boiling. Wet the pudding bag or cloth in the boiling water, and dust it liberally with flour or grease your pudding bowl or mold. Sift together dry ingredients. Stir into them the melted shortening, sugar, and raisins. Then add water to the dough and mix well. The dough should be fairly thick, but not stiff. Turn into the pudding bag, tie the bag leaving room for the duff to expand, or put the duff into a greased pudding mold.

Put the bag or mold in boiling water. If in a bag, boil for four hours; if in a mold, steam for 2 hours. You can test for doneness as you would for a cake by inserting a tester or thin bladed knife. If it comes out clean the pudding is done. When done, turn it out of the cloth onto a serving dish. Let it stand a moment to set up.

Slice it and serve with molasses, or the lemon sauce described on page 128.

Yields 12 servings.

HARDTACK OR SHIP'S BISCUIT

Hardtack, or ship's biscuit or ship's bread as it was known, was manufactured by early American bakers in seaport towns. Home bakers also made it. It most resembles the modern Maryland beaten biscuit. Made chiefly of water, flour, and the least bit of shortening, it was pounded, rolled, pricked, and cut, baked, and packed in barrels. To eat it, sailors had to soak it in their coffee, tea, or water, or in the cooking water accompanying their boiled meat.

Hardtack is still sold in Nova Scotian and Newfoundland grocery stores. Pick up a few bags on your next vacation to the Canadian maritime provinces to use in your seafarers dishes. Don't worry about it getting stale, hardtack keeps as well today as it did in the last century. You can also shop for it online.

If you wish to make your own hard tack, here is a recipe to follow.

2 cups of all purpose flour with two tablespoons of whole wheat flour mixed in.
2 teaspoons of salt
1 cup of water

Preheat the oven to 350°. Mix the flour, salt and water together, adding the water a little at a time, and adding only enough to allow a very stiff dough to result. Roll out the dough and cut the biscuits with a round cutter. Prick the tops with a fork and bake the crackers until they are hard, reducing the temperature if necessary to keep them from burning.

DANDYFUNK

...a pan of "dandyfunk," a baked mass of hard tack and molasses, a great delicacy with us and possible only at rare intervals when Chow would permit us to take up the space in his galley range....for once [we] enjoyed a complete meal of our favorite dessert.

From *Under Sail,* by Felix Riesenberg, 1919

A rough canvas bag was made into which hard ship's biscuits were placed; then we hammered the bag on the windlass until the contents were converted into what we termed flour. Next we courted the cook...offering to "wash up" for him all his greasy slushy pans,...in return for which voluntary service we secured a pinch of ground ginger, and the loan of a shallow square baking pan....We emptied the contents of the canvas bag,...mixed this with slush purloined from the tin containing the awful stuff we used for greasing down the masts....we added a little salt water until a lovely dough resulted, when it was flattened out in the baking-pan, and placed in the oven until nicely browned.

From *Seafaring,* by George Boughton, 1926

DANDYFUNK WAS A sailor-made treat. Hardtack was often freely available to the sailors, and if they could negotiate with the cook for additional ingredients and oven space they could make this item for themselves. While there seems to have been some variation in the mixture, it was always made from hardtack pounded into crumbs. Shortening or molasses could also be included. Shortening varied widely in quality on board ship; the chances of it being rancid were very good. Molasses was usually rationed, so sailors saved a bit out of their daily whack, or serving, to accumulate a supply of it for dandyfunk.

Felix Riesenberg sailed on the *A.J. Fuller* from New York to Honolulu as a foremast hand in 1897. George Boughton recounted his trip in the bark *Archos* from Sunderland, Scotland, which began in 1882 when he was 12 years old. Boughton romanticized his sailing past, so we may have to take his "recipe" for dandyfunk with a grain of salt.

Dandyfunk has the texture of a sweet cracker-crumb crust. It seems to be related to shortbreads, and examples of fat, molasses, and flour confections can be found in traditional recipes from Newfoundland. Recipes also exist in nineteenth-century cookbooks and manuscript sources for cake made with salt pork. These kinds of examples may have provided a prototype for sailors' dandyfunk.

I don't know why you would want to make this, but here is an adapted recipe in case you do. One cake of hardtack will pound out to about 1/2 to 2/3 of a cup of crumbs. The following recipe can be multiplied by the number of pieces of hardtack you use. If you cannot get hardtack, substitute the cracker with the least fat in it that you can find. Vegetable shortening is the best tasting, but miscellaneous drippings are most authentic. I don't like it at all made with water, à la Boughton, but if you want to try it that way add a 1/4 cup of lightly salted water to the recipe below.

1 piece of hardtack
   or 2/3 cup of pilot cracker crumbs
1 tablespoon shortening
2 tablespoons molasses

Preheat oven to 350°. Pound the hardtack until most crumbs are about the size of a grain of cooked rice. (There will be considerable variation as some of the hardtack becomes flour-like while other pieces remain larger.) Mix in the shortening until it is evenly blended, then add the molasses and stir to mix well.

Bake in a small greased pan in a hot oven for 15 to 20 minutes, until the molasses is all bubbly and the mixture is nicely browned. Eat warm.

LOBSCOUCE

The cook had just made for us a mess of hot "scouce"—that is, biscuit pounded fine, salt beef cut into small pieces, and a few potatoes, boiled up together and seasoned with pepper.

From *Two Years Before the Mast,* by Richard Henry Dana, 1834, World Classics Edition

The steward was bringing up the refuse food of the cabin...I got a panful of "scouce" as it is called, and a biscuit. The scouce is a curious mixture, onions, pepper, potatoes, several kinds of meat & everything eatable in the ship....Scouce for the forecastle is made of bread & meat soaked in water & then boiled.

From John Perkins's *Journal at Sea,* 1845

1 lb. salt meat cubed
1 med. onion
2 tbsp. rice
1 cup each of diced carrots, turnips, and potatoes
1 parsnip (diced)
1 cup chopped cabbage

Soak meat overnight to remove the salt. Drain. Add 6 or 7 cups of fresh cold water, and cook for one hour. Then add the vegetables and rice. Cook until vegetables are tender. (Spareribs may be used instead of salt meat.)

Lobscouce is a very thick soup or stew of vegetables and salt meat, A native of Liverpool, England, to this day is often called a "Lob-Saucer," so this is probably where this recipe originated. It has been used in Newfoundland for at least 70 years.

Recipe submitted by Netta Ivany of Sunnyside, Newfoundland, and Miss Alice Lacey of Wesleyville, Newfoundland, *Fat Back and Molasses: a Collection of Favorite Old Recipes from Newfoundland and Labrador,* by the Rev. Ivan Jesperson, 1974

HERE ARE TWO VERSIONS of scouce: a simple one suitable for the fo'c'sle crew, and a more elaborate one for the cabin. The Newfoundland recipe is a cabin as well as a landsman's version. Miss Lacey and Ms. Ivany are right about the origin of lobscouce: it is a common dish in northern England, associated with Liverpool in particular, and Liverpool's connection with the sea may explain why scouce appeared so often in the fo'c'sles of British and American ships.

Lobscouce tastes good. Sailors regarded it as a particular treat, and it certainly required more effort by the cook because he had to chop meat and potatoes, and break up sea biscuits. How carefully he did that determined how good the scouce would be. Potatoes were not always included in fo'c'sle scouce, but might have been if it were made on a day when beef and potatoes were on the mess bill. The hardtack absorbed some of the liquid and thickened the whole thing.

Neither salt meat, particularly beef, nor hardtack are commonly available today. If you wish to produce an approximation of salt beef, purchase a cheap cut of beef, rub it thoroughly with pickling salt, and set it in a cool, dry place for a month or more. Check it frequently and add salt as needed.

At sea the beef would have been freshened in the harness cask; be sure to soak your beef at least overnight. The interpretation below is for a fo'c'sle scouce. For a cabin-style scouce use the Newfoundland recipe below.

1 pound salt meat, cubed
2 cups water
4 potatoes, cubed
1/2 cake of hardtack, broken up fairly small
Pepper to taste

Put the meat and water in a heavy pot, and stew it covered over a medium heat until the meat is cooked through. Add the potatoes (and other vegetables) and cook it, still covered, until tender. Add the hardtack and pepper, reduce the heat, and simmer uncovered until the scouce has thickened.

Serves 4.

SPOTTED DICK

The pudding was a mixture of a cupful of flour and a cupful of suet, a cupful of currants, an egg, and a little milk to mix. It was a boiled dumpling pudding ... boiled in a cloth.

From Recipes from an *Old Farmhouse*, by Alison Uttley, 1966

PATRICK O'BRIAN always calls this pudding a spotted "dog" but there is no historical precedence that I can find for that term. This recipe is very close to a duff, see page 198, except it uses suet and has a great many currants.

You can use the proportions provided above. Boil it in a cloth or put into a greased pudding bowl or mold, and steam for an hour and a half. A tester inserted should come out clean, just as for cake. Serve it warm, and for a sauce, use melted jelly or jam as for the roly-poly pudding.

Serves 6-8 generously.

FISHERMAN'S BREWIS

Salt fish as required Hard bread as required Fat Pork as Required

To prepare Bread: Split cakes of hard bread; allow 1 cake per person. Place in large saucepan well covered with water. Soak overnight. The next day, using same water bring to near boil. (do not boil)

Drain immediately. Keep hot. To prepare fish, soak salt fish overnight, changing water once. Boil for 20 minutes until fish is flaky. Drain and remove skin and bones from fish. Combine fish and hard bread together. Serve with scrunchions (small cubes of fat pork fried to golden brown).

Annie Mugford, Clarkes Beach, Newfoundland. From *Fat Back and Molasses: A Collection of Favorite Recipes* from Newfoundland and Labrador, by Rev. Ivan Jesperson, 1974

READING THE RECIPE for fish and brewis ("broos") will raise for many the specters of hypertension and cholesterol problems. But it is perfectly delicious, which amazed those who tested it and thought that soaked hardbread would be all mushy (it holds its shape very well) and the notion that it would either be too salty or bland (it was neither). The secret is the salt pork, which you must use.

Soaked hardtack swells considerably, and in the following recipe it out-bulks the codfish quite a bit. Adjust it to your taste; you can make a perfectly good fish and brewis with half a cake per person. Salt cod, which in some places you can buy whole, with bones in and skin on, varies in weight, but allow at least one pound for four to six servings and you will have plenty left over for hash.

A friend who lived for a while on Fogo Island, Newfoundland, reports that her neighbors cautioned her against boiling the brewis. It is to be cooked gently:

"You brews the brewis," they told her.

1 lb. boned salt codfish
1/2 to 1 cake hardtack per person
1/2 to 3/4 lb. salt pork

The night before you intend to serve fish and brewis, put the hardtack in a deep bowl and cover it well with water. Put the cod in another bowl and cover with water. Soak overnight.

The next day change the water on the codfish and let it soak until mealtime. When you are ready to prepare the dish, put the hardtack (brewis) on to cook over low to medium heat, allowing it to simmer only. Meanwhile, cut the salt pork into small pieces and fry over a low heat till the bits of fat are all golden brown. While the salt pork is cooking, put the fish in fresh water and cook till it is flaky (about 10 minutes).

Drain the brewis, and break it up into smaller pieces. Flake the fish apart and mix into the brewis. Add pepper to taste.

Put on a platter and drizzle all the salt pork fat over the fish and brewis and sprinkle the crispy salt pork "scrunchions" on top.

Yields 4-6 very hearty servings.

ROLY-POLY PUDDING

Readers of the popular Patrick O'Brian novels about the adventures of Jack Aubrey and Stephen Maturin may wonder about some of Aubrey's favorite dishes. Roly-poly pudding was one. A simple steamed pudding, made of a biscuit-like dough spread with jam and rolled up for boiling in a cloth, roly-poly was a simple pudding common among ordinary folks of the eighteenth and nineteenth centuries in Britain and America.

Some roly-polys were filled with sliced apples or other fresh fruit, others simply used jams or jellies. Most people prefer to bake it. The following recipe is adapted from a modern English recipe and calls for grated suet. You can actually use your favorite biscuit recipe, substituting water for milk.

2 cups of flour
1 tablespoon of baking powder
2 tablespoons of sugar
3/4 cup grated suet
2/3 cup water
About a half pint of strawberry or
**   raspberry jam, or your favorite**
**   preserves.**

Preheat the oven to 375° and grease a baking sheet. Sift the dry ingredients together into a bowl, and rub in the suet until the mixture is well blended. Add the water, and toss until a soft, biscuit-like dough forms. Knead it a few times on a floured board, then roll out into a rough rectangle with a floured rolling pin until it is about quarter of an inch thick. Spread the dough's surface with the jam leaving one jam-less border about 2 inches wide. Starting with the jam spread border, roll the dough up toward the plain border. Pinch the dough shut on the long edge and at the ends. Bake for 25 minutes or until risen and golden flecked.

Slice to serve, and melt more jam or jelly to use as a sauce.

Serves 6-8.

TOASTED CHEESE

Another of Jack Aubrey's favorites is toasted cheese which his steward Killick fixes for him. At its simplest, it is cheese melted on bread under the broiler. There are other recipes in which cheese is grated or pounded with mustard and beer or ale or even a bit of cayenne added, before the mixture is spread on bread or toast and heated to soften the cheese. Other versions resemble Welsh Rarebit.

If you are planning a dinner party around a hearth cooked meal, this is an ideal hors d'ouvre. Use a sharp cheddar, grate it, and beat in a few tablespoons of beer or ale, and mustard to taste, until you have a spreadable consistency. Spread it on toasted bread, and using your salamander or a coal shovel heated in the fireplace embers, heat the top until it is bubbly.

12 Confections

CONFECTIONS IN THE PAST included preserved fruits and sugar-coated nuts and seeds, but were usually not found outside the wealthy classes. For most of the nineteenth century, candy making was the province of confectionary shops that made and sold candy sticks, sour balls, and other sweets in addition to making ice cream and some baked goods. With cheaper sugar and molasses in the 1800s, even the middle class could enjoy candy making at home, and by the end of the century, a variety of taffy and fudge joined homemade brittles and sugared peels. There is even evidence of at least one captain's wife making candy aboard ship.

MOLASSES CANDY

1 cup New Orleans molasses
1 cup of brown sugar
1 tablespoonful of vinegar
1 ounce of melted butter

Mix all together, and boil without stirring until it hardens when dropped in cold water; then add a teaspoonful of baking soda, and pour into buttered tins.

Or, when cool, pull and cut into sticks. While pulling, brush the hands with butter or moisten them with ice water.

From *Mrs. Rorer's Philadelphia Cook Book,* 1886

WITH HER RECIPE for molasses candy, Mrs. Rorer spun out recipes for peanut and walnut candy, by instructing for walnut candy to "Make a plain molasses candy, and, when done, grease deep pans with butter, fill nearly full with walnut kernel, pour the molasses candy over them, and stand away to cool." Her recipe for peanut candy was "Peanut molasses candy made precisely the same as Walnut Molasses Candy."

The same mixture can be used to bind popped corn to make popcorn balls.

This three-in-one recipe will give you two sorts of nut brittles plus a hard molasses candy. All have a sturdy molasses flavor. The peanut candy should be made with roasted peanuts. When pulled and snipped into pieces, the molasses candy has a lovely golden-brown satiny appearance and sticks wonderfully to the teeth.

1 cup molasses
1 cup light brown sugar
1 tablespoon vinegar
2 tablespoons of butter
1 teaspoon baking soda

Mix together the molasses, brown sugar, vinegar, and butter. Set it to boil till it reaches the hard ball stage or 270° on a candy thermometer. Remove from the heat and stir in baking soda. The candy will foam up and change color. Pour onto a greased cookie sheet, and when cool enough to handle, and working quickly, pull it as you would for taffy, folding it back on itself a few times until it is almost too stiff to pull. Stretch it into sticks and snip the pieces off with kitchen scissors, allowing them to cool on waxed paper. Wrap them in waxed paper, if you wish. Store in an airtight container.

PEANUT OR WALNUT MOLASSES CANDY

3 cups roasted peanuts or walnut pieces
1 batch of molasses candy
(recipe on previous page)

Mix together the molasses, brown sugar, vinegar, and butter. Set it to boil till it reaches the hard ball stage or 270° on a candy thermometer. While the syrup is boiling, butter a large baking pan or a cookie sheet. (I recommend the cookie sheet because it is easier to break the candy up into chunks when it is in thinner sheets.) As soon as the syrup reaches 270° on a candy thermometer, remove from the heat and stir in 1 teaspoon baking soda. The candy will foam up and change color. Pour the candy over the nuts in the pan, spreading with a greased spatula to cover the nuts as evenly as possible. Set aside to cool. When the candy has cooled and hardened, break up into smaller pieces and store in an airtight container.

POPCORN BALLS

The versatile molasses candy recipe above can be added to popped corn, and formed into balls. Nineteenth-century narratives and diaries mention popcorn as a treat and Sallie, wife of Captain Fred Smith tells us she made popcorn balls for the crew of the *John P. West* for Christmas in 1882, but there are very few historic recipes for preparing them. One calls for gum arabic and suggests various combinations of white and brown sugar and molasses.

The ingredients for Mrs. Rorer's molasses candy would all have been available on shipboard. Mrs. Smith could have used an even simpler molasses and vinegar mixture boiled to just under a hard crack stage. Following are instructions for making popcorn balls with molasses candy. Half a cup of corn will yield about three quarts of popped corn. This recipe is now a personal favorite and I make popcorn balls for Halloween and Christmas both. I prefer the molasses flavor, and modern corn-syrup-based popcorn balls taste bland to me.

8 quarts popped corn
1 batch of molasses candy from
(recipe on previous page)

Pop enough corn to yield 8 quarts. Keep warm in a large pan in the oven while you prepare the molasses candy. As soon as the candy reaches 270° on a candy thermometer, stir in the baking soda to mix. Working quickly, pour the candy over the popcorn, stirring to coat the popcorn evenly. Butter your hands, and shape handfuls of the coated corn into the size ball you like best. If the mixture gets too hard to work, set it in the oven a moment to soften slightly, then continue. (Better yet, get a friend or a couple of children to help you.) Set the balls on a greased cookie sheet to cool.

Yields 18-24 balls about 3-4 inches in diameter.

13Beverages

HERE ARE A SMATTERING OF DRINKABLES, not intended to be a comprehensive list of nineteenth-century beverages. A few are suitable for households run on the Temperance model and a few are for those who like to relax with a drink of whiskey or rum. Some cookbooks in the 1800s only held recipes for coffee, tea, and chocolate. Others provided punch recipes, and advised on the choice of wines to do with various menus. A great many New Englanders did eschew alcohol, but quite a few thought there was no harm in a sociable glass.

Sailors at sea were often unwilling Temperance adherents, and groused that the Temperance was all in the fo'c'sle. Too often that was true. Cheap-skate Yankee ship owners released from the obligation to provide the time honored gill of rum once considered indispensable, were happy to eliminate rum from the store carried aboard for the crew. What happened in the cabin was up to the captain, who sometimes provided whiskey and rum for his own use and for medicinal use by the crew.

SWANKY OR SWITCHEL

HARVEST DRINK

Mix with five gallons of good water, half a gallon of molasses, one quart of vinegar, and two ounces of powdered ginger. This will make not only a very pleasant beverage, but one highly invigorating and healthful.

From *Practical American Cookery and Domestic Economy*, by Miss Hall, 1855

THE SWANKY was served aboard fishing vessels a kind of seagoing switchel, which Miss Hall describes above as "a harvest drink." Similar in purpose to modern sports drinks, it slakes thirst and provides a bit of sugar energy. Molasses is high in minerals as well. This recipe yields close to six gallons, which would be about right for a crew of people haying in summer months or a schooner full of handliners. One of our testers remarked that the swanky "tastes like something that's good for you." You may want to sample it after mixing and add additional water to taste.

5 cups water
1/2 cup of molasses
1/4 cup of vinegar
3 teaspoons of ginger

Mix and chill. Taste and adjust water to taste.

Yields about a quart and a half.

RASPBERRY SHRUB

Raspberry shrub mixed with water is a pure, delicious drink for summer; and in a country where raspberries are abundant it is a good economy to make it answer instead of Port and Catalonia wine. Put raspberries in a pan, and scarcely cover them with strong vinegar. Add a pint of sugar to a pint of juice. ... scald it, skim it, and bottle it when cold.

From *American Frugal Housewife*, Lydia Maria Child, 1833

SHRUB WAS, in the eighteenth-century, a punch-like beverage made with sugar, oranges or lemon, and rum. This shrub is essentially raspberry vinegar made into a sweet syrup and was a popular nineteenth-century Temperance alternative to alcoholic drinks. It makes a lovely summer drink as Mrs. Child promised, though modern folks can mix it with club soda and pour it over ice cubes. You can use currants, blackberries, and strawberries in this recipe, too.

2 cups of ripe raspberries
Cider vinegar just to cover
Sugar

Put the raspberries into a glass jar. Add the vinegar just to cover the berries. Let stand for a week or so, until the vinegar is a deep color, and the berries have faded. Strain out the berries and measure the vinegar, and put it into a heavy stainless steel pan. Now add to the vinegar an equal amount of sugar. (For every cup of vinegar, use one cup of sugar.) Bring the mixture to a boil; the sugar should all dissolve, and a syrup results. Allow to cool and store in a jar or bottle. Refrigeration is not required. To serve, put some into a glass with ice cubes and add soda or water until you have your desired flavor.

COFFEE

We always measured our coffee in a glass that held exactly a quarter of a pound. We poured water into our pot up to a certain mark inside; it made eight mugs. I think the biggest factor was the old blue agate pot that would hold maybe two gallons. It had the essence of coffee in it, like a pipe carries tobacco. Soap never touched it; when it was time to make new coffee, we rinsed it overboard to dispose of the old grounds and some drops of sea water clung to it that helped to give it a flavor. We brought the water to a boil, poured in the coffee, and moved it off the flame. We had a long-handled wooden spoon that we beat it up with for a minute or two. Then we crushed up an egg in the hand and dropped it in, shell and all; that settled the grounds. After settin' for three, four minutes, it was ready to pour.

From *Charlie York: Maine Coast Fisherman*, by Harold B. Clifford, 1974

THIS IS CHARLIE YORK'S "recipe" for the coffee that he made aboard his fishing boat, the *Fish Hawk*, in the early 1930s at Boothbay, Maine. The coffee was served with canned milk and sugar. The coffee made such an impression on a visiting doctor from New York City that he bet a friend that it would be the best coffee his friend ever had—and the doctor won the bet.

A quarter of a pound of coffee to two quarts of water is a good proportion, assuming that Charlie's mugs held a standard eight ounces of water.

LEMONADE

Good lemonade can be made with half a pint of lemon juice extracted with a squeezer, and strained), three pints of water and a generous pint of sugar. Have the drink cold.

From *Miss Parloa's New Cook Book,* by Maria Parloa, 1880

Millions of lemons have been squeezed on behalf of Temperance since the 1830s or so. Next to water, lemonade was the drink of choice for those attempting to reform American drinking habits. If you make your lemonade from scratch, you will find that bar sugar dissolves more readily in beverages than regular granulated sugar does; you can make your own bar sugar by whirling granulated sugar in the blender for a few moments. Or you can make a syrup of the water and sugar by heating them together until the sugar dissolves. Cool the syrup before adding the lemon juice.

1 cup of freshly squeezed lemon juice
6 cups of water
2 cups of sugar.

Mix together until the sugar is dissolved.

Makes 2 quarts.

WHISKEY PUNCH

Whiskey's the fellah,—said the young man John.—Make it into a punch, cold at dinner-time, 'n' hot at bed-time. I'll come up and show you how to mix it....real Burbon's (sic) the stuff. Hot water, sugar, 'n' jest a little shavin' of lemon-skin in it,—skin, mind you, none o' your juice; take it off thin,—shape of one of them flat curls the factory-girls wear on the sides of their foreheads.

From "The Professor at the Breakfast-Table. What He Said, What He Heard, and What He Saw," *Atlantic Monthly* (June 1859)

THIS RECIPE FOR whiskey punch comes from a regular *Atlantic Monthly* column written tongue-in-cheek about what the "Professor" hears discussed at his boardinghouse breakfast table. The topic *du jour* happened to be a cough plaguing one of the boarders. Whiskey punch was the recommended medication.

Many will agree with the young man John who says that "real Burbon's the stuff"—though, of course, a very good whiskey punch can be made from Irish and Scotch whiskies. This is a very agreeable drink whether you have a cough or not. When you make a whiskey punch, plan to mix the drink in a heatproof mug or glass. The amount of water and sugar are really a matter of opinion and taste; mix in the same proportion as you favor for whiskey and water. Nowadays you will want to wash the lemon before skinning off a curl of peel, and put it into the glass or mug before you add the hot water.

FISH HOUSE PUNCH

This very sweet and potent punch is pretty typical of the sweetened rum and citrus based punches, often called shrub, common in early America. A political club named The State of Schuylkill, established in eighteenth-century Philadelphia, is generally identified as the source of the punch named for their meeting place.

You can use club soda or cold tea in the place of the water.

3 cups of lemon juice, sweetened to taste
1-1/2 pints brandy
1 pint peach brandy
2 pints of light rum
1 quart of water or more to taste

Mix gently, and pour over ice in a punch bowl or serve in old fashioned glasses with ice.

INDEX

LIST OF ILLUSTRATIONS

Cover image by an unknown artist from The Ella Gallup Sumner and Mary Catlin Sumner Collection, Wadsworth Atheneum, Hartford, Connecticut

P. 26. This party is waiting for their chowder to cook on the granite coast of New Hampshire about 1890. A tripod, a kettle and a fire were all that the feast required.
(Photo from The Sandler Collection)

P. 81. Fishermen are shown dressing their catch at Biddeford Pool, Maine, ca. 1884. A typical workday scene in a New England fishing community.
(Baldwin Coolidge photo, MSM 79.18.1)

P. 86. Fish flakes like these at Provincetown, Massachusetts, covered acres of fishing communities in the last half of the 1800s. The salted and still-wet fish were laid out to dry in the air, carefully tended and covered in case of rain, and left on the flakes until dry enough to store for extended periods and perhaps be made into various dried-fish products.
(Stereograph by Nickerson, Provincetown, MSM 79.176.1)

P. 102. The popularity of oysters meant that they were quickly depleted in southern New England. By the mid-1880s, one writer described oystering as more of a farming than fishing operation. Seed oysters imported from the Chesapeake were "planted" on beds of culch – old oyster shells – where the spawn settled and young oysters grew. Later the oysters might be replanted in deeper water until they were a marketable size.
(Lithograph advertisement, MSM 80.107.16)

P. 104. This poster with its smiling oyster faces only begins to convey the extreme popularity of oysters in the nineteenth century. It was the seafood most consistently mentioned in cook books both coastwise and inland in the latter 1800s. As the oyster "Express" hints, shucked and packed oysters were carried inland by rail to be enjoyed hundreds of miles from Oyster Point, in New Haven, and other places along the southern New England shore where they were tonged out of the beds.
(Blockprint, 1880, courtesy of New Haven Colony Historical Society)

P. 135. The highly appropriate title of this image is "Women Enjoying a Seated Tea While Making a Strong Stand in Favor of Temperance."
(Woodcut ca. 1840, Albert Alden Proof Book, courtesy American Antiquarian Society)

P. 162. A quartet of doughnut-eaters on a picnic around the turn of the century are having a very good time.
(Glass-plate photograph by Edward H. Newbury, MSM 80.41.446)

P. 176. Photograph from The American Antiquarian Society, Worcester, Massachusetts.

P. 197. This mess bill from the brig Reaper from the Manuscripts Collection of Mystic Seaport shows the menu that repeated weekly.
(MSM 92-7-5)

P. 201. From this galley located at the starboard-side stern quarter of the *Charles W. Morgan*, the whaleship's books prepared three meals a day.
(MSM 55-1-14)

ABOUT THE AUTHOR

Sandra Oliver, a Connecticut native, began working with food history at Mystic Seaport in 1971 when she developed the Buckingham-Hall House fireplace cooking program. She began work on *Saltwater Foodways: New Englanders and Their Food at Sea and Ashore in 1985* and won the Jane Grigson Award for Distinguished Scholarship in the Julia Child Cookbook Awards sponsored by the International Association of Culinary Professionals. Since then she has co-authored *Giving Thanks: Thanksgiving History and Recipes from Pilgrims to Pumpkin Pie* and *Food in Colonial and Federal America*. For nearly two decades she has been the publisher and editor of *Food History News*, a quarterly newsletter dedicated to North American food history. She travels and speaks across the country on American food history. Sandy and her husband Jamie MacMillan, live in Islesboro, Maine, maintain a large garden, raise pigs and chickens which blends the best of the past and present.